WITHDRAWN

BIAS IN HUMAN REASONING: CAUSES AND CONSEQUENCES

BIAS IN HUMAN REASONING: CAUSES AND CONSEQUENCES

Jonathan St. B. T. Evans

Professor of Cognitive Psychology
Polytechnic SW, England

LEA LAWRENCE ERLBAUM ASSOCIATES, PUBLISHERS LEA
Hove and London (UK)   Hillsdale (USA)

CALVIN T. RYAN LIBRARY
KEARNEY STATE COLLEGE
KEARNEY, NEBRASKA

Copyright © 1989 by Lawrence Erlbaum Associates Ltd.
  All rights reserved. No part of this book may be reproduced in
any form, by photostat, microform, retrieval system, or any
other means, without the prior written permission of the
publisher.

Lawrence Erlbaum Associates Ltd., Publishers
27 Palmeira Mansions
Church Road
Hove
East Sussex, BN3 2FA
U.K.

British Library Cataloguing in Publication Data

Evans, Jonathan St. B.T., *1948-*
  Bias in human reasoning: causes and consequences.
  (Essays in cognitive psychology)
  1. Man. Deductive reasoning. Psychological aspects
  I. Title   II. Series
  153.4'33

  ISBN 0-86377-106-8

Typeset by Clear Image Ltd., London EC1
Printed and bound by BPCC Wheaton, Exeter

Contents

Foreword

My interest in the psychology of reasoning dates from the late 1960s when, as an undergraduate student at University College London, I attended a research seminar delivered by Peter Wason—subsequently to supervise my PhD on conditional reasoning. My concern with the topic of *bias* in human reasoning also has its origins in this period for two main reasons. The first was the pioneering work of Peter Wason who, despite the prevailing rationalism and dominant Piagetian theory of the time, was conducting experiments on ingenious inductive and deductive reasoning tasks of his own devising which looked easy, but induced error in the great majority of intelligent subjects who attempted them. These tasks, known as the "2 4 6" problem and the selection task, have survived as major paradigms for the study of human reasoning until the present day and are discussed at some length within this book.

The second origin of my interest in bias was pure chance. In my early experiments on reasoning with conditional statements I decided to investigate sentences with negative components—for what reason I cannot now recall. The consequence was that this manipulation did not simply increase errors but introduced systematic biases which sometimes helped and sometimes hindered subjects from achieving the logical solution to the problems set. These effects were neither expected nor predicted but having found them, I naturally wanted to try to understand why they occurred. In my later, as in my earlier experiments on reasoning, I did not need to go looking for biases—a variety of types of systematic and reliable error continued to appear in my data.

Over the past 20 years a number of important changes have occurred in the psychological study of human reasoning. The logical/rational view of human reasoning has weakened its grip considerably, although some theorists of this type remain to the present day. Whilst reasoning research in the 1960s was divorced from other cognitive research on memory and attention, the field has become much better integrated into mainstream cognitive psychology and subject to the same fads and fashions. Hence, stress on mental representations and process models flourished in the 1970s and integrative cognitive theories based on schemas and mental models have been increasingly promoted in the 1980s. All the while, the rapidly expanding literature reporting experimental research on human reasoning has continued to amass evidence of error and bias for the theorists to explain—or in some cases explain away—and for philosophers to debate with regard to the implications for human rationality.

Research in the fields of behavioural decision theory and statistical inference developed in a parallel but largely independent way over the same period. What was a relatively small field dominated in the 1960s by Bayesian psychologists with a predominantly rationalistic view of human inference, was transformed during the 1970s and 1980s to a field principally concerned with the demonstration and explanation of bias in human inference. This transformation was due in large part to a series of quite extraordinarily stimulating and high-quality papers by Amos Tversky and Daniel Kahneman who demonstrated many fallacies in judgements and inferences about probabilistic events. They also strongly challenged the earlier view of people as "intuitive statisticians", suggesting instead that we rely on simple heuristic rules of thumb for such judgements. This work has had a major impact in both cognitive and social psychology as well as on a number of other disciplines such as economics and management science.

From a personal point of view, I started to develop interest in the topic of statistical inference in the mid-1970s, and have conducted parallel research on deductive and statistical reasoning since that period. Whilst personally convinced of the essential connection between the two traditions in terms of the psychology of the underlying thinking, I have observed with some dismay that the two fields have continued largely on their separate courses with only a small amount of cross-referencing or attempts at joint reviewing appearing in the journals. Indeed, my wish to demonstrate the close connection of the two fields and explore the possibility of a common theoretical approach to the phenomena they concern was a major motivation for the writing of this book.

This is the second book on the psychology of reasoning that I have written, but it is by no means simply an update of the earlier one. In *The Psychology of Deductive Reasoning* (1982, Routledge and Kegan Paul) I set out to write a text book with eclectic coverage of research on deductive reasoning conducted to that time. In contrast, the present volume is an extended essay intended to describe, explain, and consider the consequences of bias in human reasoning, with the scope widened beyond that of deductive reasoning to include studies of inductive and statistical inference as well. The coverage of literature is necessarily selective although I have tried to discuss most of the biases which have caused particular interest in these fields in recent years. No such selective exercise can please everyone, however. Several reviewers of the manuscript of this book suggested other topics that I might have included—but they all had different preferences about what to add. Had I accommodated them all, the book would have been a very extended essay indeed!

Whilst including a number of detailed reviews of topics of current interest in the psychology of human inference, this book should, then, be read for what it is: a personal perspective on the issue of reasoning bias. I have attempted to classify the main types of bias, to make comparisons between work on different aspects of human inference, to provide a specific explanation of biases within a general theoretical framework, and finally to consider some of the practical applications of research in this field. The extent to which I have succeeded in these aims is for others to judge.

Whilst I must accept sole responsibility for the ideas presented in this book, there are a number of other psychologists whose contribution to my thinking on the topic should be acknowledged. Firstly, I must express my gratitude to Peter Wason not only for his original stimulation of my personal interest in human inference but also for his pioneering study of error and bias in reasoning. I would also like to thank Phil Johnson-Laird for a particularly detailed and helpful reading of the draft manuscript of this book, as well as for the many stimulating arguments about reasoning theory that he has given me over the years. I have, of course, benefited also from numerous discussions with colleagues and collaborators, some of whom also provided critical readings of the manuscript. In particular I would like to acknowledge Steve Newstead, Paul Pollard, Ken Manktelow, Richard Griggs, Julie Barston, Phil Brooks and Ian Dennis.

1 Introduction

Human intelligence is a remarkable thing. Every one of us, every day, routinely performs a host of intelligent actions which still largely defeat the most sophisticated computer programs which experts in artificial intelligence have been able to devise. We glance around us and instantly construct a detailed, three dimensional and largely accurate perception of the surrounding world. We talk to a friend, effortlessly extracting the intended meaning of their utterances from the pattern of activity in the air molecules reaching our ears, and constructing a sensible reply from the infinite number of linguistically sound alternatives available. We attend to problems, retrieving from our vast stores of memory just those items relevant to the matter in question. We pursue our lives through the conduct of hundreds of plans at different levels and in different stages of completion, from making a cup of coffee to pursuing a 30-year career plan—and, by and large, manage to be in the right place doing the right thing at the right time.

And yet, of course, we make mistakes. We propose solutions to problems, generate forecasts of the future and decide courses of action on the basis of our judgement of a situation. When we get it wrong, the consequences can be costly, even disastrous. Someone decided to market the thalidomide drug; someone else judged the experiment with the Chernobyl reactor to be safe. Poor judgement by a senior manager may put the company out of business and by a finance minister might depress a whole nation's economy. Faulty reasoning by a scientist might delay the discovery of important new knowledge and lead to inaccurate applications of existing work. And so on, and so on.

Clearly the quality of someone's thinking cannot be judged simply by its outcome, although there is a human tendency to be wise after the event. A

1

recent example in the United Kingdom occurred when a massive storm hit southern England in the autumn of 1987 causing immense damage. Strong public criticism was immediately directed at the Meteorological Office for failing to predict the event. An official enquiry subsequently vindicated the forecasters, since the storm developed in a freak manner and in a sea area largely uncovered by weather reporting facilities. In the wake of a disaster, people appear generally to believe that steps should have been taken to avoid it, even if its *a priori* probability was very low (the 1987 storm, for example, was a one-in-400-years event). In this case the poor thinking would appear to be manifest in the public reaction rather than in the forecasters themselves (see Chapter Five for a discussion of "hindsight bias").

This example illustrates two reasons why bad consequences might not reflect bad thinking—insufficient data and the impracticality of catering for very improbable events. This is not, of course, to say that errors of human reasoning and judgement may not also be responsible for many of the poor decisions that affect us. A massive amount of psychological research into human thinking, reasoning and judgement has been conducted, especially in the past 20 years or so. Although there are difficulties in defining criteria for correct performance on such tasks—which I shall discuss later—these studies have resulted in widespread reporting of a host of systematic errors, or *biases* as they are usually called.

Just as bad consequences do not necessarily reflect bad thinking, so good decisions may not reflect sound reasoning. For example, where a bias to respond on the basis of a logically irrelevant feature of a task exists, it may on some occasions produce a result which coincides with the logically prescribed choice. Hence, one cannot simply decide whether or not people are competent to perform an inference by assessing their performance on a single type of problem incorporating the principle. It is necessary to investigate reasoning when a number of features of the form and content of the problems are varied, in order to identify the nature of the processes involved, and the extent and nature of any biases which may be operating.

This book is concerned with discussion of a representative sample of the reasoning biases which have been identified in the research literatures concerned. The motivation for the book is both theoretical and applied. The first theoretical objective is to classify the major types of bias, relating work across several distinct literatures which normally proceed with little cross-referencing. This aim is reflected in the content of Chapters Two to Five which are organised not by the experimental paradigm studied, but by the nature of the phenomena observed. For example, in Chapter Two, evidence of selective processing biases is examined in a range of reasoning tasks from deductive reasoning to statistical judgement. The second theoretical objective which is pursued throughout the book is an attempt to explain the causes of the major types of bias identified and to understand them within a general theoretical framework which is presented, in outline, at the end of this chapter. The applied objective—for which theoretical understanding is required—is to consider the practical consequences for real life problem solving and decision making and to discuss means of reducing the impact of biases via educational and other approaches. This "debiasing" problem, as it is sometimes called, will be the focus of Chapter Six.

THE NATURE OF REASONING TASKS

A classical distinction is that between inductive and deductive reasoning. A deductive inference involves an attempt to infer conclusions from propositions held to be true but does not increase the semantic information in the process: the conclusions merely state explicitly information already latent in the premises. Logic, a sub-discipline of philosophy, is concerned with prescribing correct procedures for deductive inference based upon the principle of *necessity*. In essence this means that for a conclusion to be inferred as valid it must not only be consistent with the premises of the argument but there must be no counter-examples to it. Suppose, for example, that I say to you: "Jane reads a lot of library books. All the library books have hard covers." You would be entitled to make the inference that Jane reads a lot of hard back books, but not to the inference that she reads *mostly* hard back books, since for all you know she may buy and read even larger quantities of paperbacks.

Inductive inferences are those which involve increasing the amount of semantic information beyond that given and are seen in modern philosophy as related to the explanation of phenomena and scientific reasoning rather than the domain of logic. One form of induction involves imputing probable causes to observed effects—as, for example, when one sees a damaged car by the roadside and presumes that a road traffic accident has recently occurred in this location. Such inferences are not logically valid, since they violate the principle of necessity—the car may have had the accident some time ago, and been driven and parked here by the indifferent owner. However, the ability to make such reasonable and plausible conjectures is obviously important in understanding the world about us.

Another common and important form of induction is that of generalisation from experience in which we infer general rules or categories from the observation of specific instances. For example, people have intuitive theories about gravity (whether or not they have studied Newton) based upon countless observations that objects without visible means of support fall to the ground. Similarly, our knowledge of concepts and categories is based upon induction. A child learns to recognise a cat and distinguish it from a dog by seeing many examples labelled by adults as one or the other and somehow inducing rules to define these categories. In natural thinking, inductions and deductions may alternate, as a provisional rule which has been induced is then applied deductively to a new example. Hence, a young child whose experience has been largely confined to cats might well overgeneralise and classify the first dog it sees as a cat. This false deduction implies possession of an incorrect rule which is consequently revised. In like manner a scientist might induce an hypothesis from the results of one experiment and test it deductively by predicting the findings of another.

Psychological research on reasoning has been influenced strongly by normative or prescriptive theories which seek to determine whether inferences are right or wrong. To describe an inference as an error, fallacy, or exhibition of a bias implies some criterion for correctness. There is nothing unusual in the use of accuracy measures in cognitive psychology. Memory experiments often involve measuring the numbers of errors made on a recognition or recall task, perceptual experiments may test for hits and misses in the detection of signals and so on. What makes reasoning research different is simply the fact that the criteria and methods of measuring accuracy are themselves controversial as we shall see later in the chapter.

In the case of deductive reasoning, as already stated, the normative theory is that of formal logic. The study of logic dates back to Aristotle who proposed a system based upon the syllogism. This is a very restricted form in which arguments have two premises involving four alternative types of proposition: All A are B, Some A are B, Some A are not B and No A are B. The conclusion of each argument links a subject and predicate each of which is related to a middle term in the two premises (see Evans, 1982, Chapter Five for a full description of syllogistic logic). An example of a syllogism is the following: Some young people are students; No students are lecturers; Therefore, some young people are not lecturers. This argument is valid—that is to say the conclusion must be true provided that the premises are true. At least one young person must be a student and therefore not a lecturer. Validity means that there is no possible state of the world in which the premises could be true and the conclusion false. It is not sufficient that the premises are consistent with the conclusion—they must necessitate it. Hence, the following syllogism is invalid: Some young people are not students; No students are lecturers; Therefore, some young people are not lecturers. The difference is that although the first premise *suggests* that some young people are lecturers, it does not necessarily imply this. Nor is one's real world knowledge that many young people are students of any relevance to assessing the logic of the argument. The premises of this argument could apply to a world in which no young people are students and all of them are lecturers—a situation in which the conclusion stated would be false.

The syllogistic form is very limited and applicable only to a restricted range of real life arguments. Consequently, philosophers have developed more powerful logics such as the propositional and predicate calculi (see Lemmon, 1965). However, most psychological experiments on deductive reasoning have involved the presentation of relatively simple arguments for evaluation, and a substantial modern literature exists on psychological study of syllogistic reasoning. Most other work on deductive reasoning involves propositional logic, especially concerning conditional statements of the form *If p then q*. An example of the kind of argument which is shown to subjects is the following: If a card has an A on the left side then it has a 4 on the right side; The card has a 7 on the right side; Therefore, the card does not have an A on the left side.

This argument is valid, as is any of the form "If p then q, not-q therefore not-p", regardless of what propositions may be substituted for p and q. This is an example of *Modus Tollens* which is often regarded as an elementary principle or inference rule which can contribute to the solution of more complex problems. The validity of *Modus Tollens* can, however, be demonstrated from the principle of necessity stated earlier. In the above example the first premise tells us that we can only consider a card with an A on the left if it also has a 4 on the right. Hence, we cannot contemplate the possibility that a card bearing a different number, 7, could have an A paired with it.

Psychological experiments on deductive reasoning often involve the presentation of arguments with the request for subjects to make a validity judgement. Sometimes subjects are given a list of alternative conclusions to choose from. Sometimes they are given no conclusions to evaluate and are asked to generate one of their own. Some reasoning tasks require subjects to consider and evaluate alternative hypotheses in a way which requires understanding of logical relationships. A famous example is the Wason selection task (Wason, 1966) aspects of which are dealt with in several chapters of this book. The results of the many hundreds of such experiments that have been reported in the psychological literature indicate that subjects' responses very frequently deviate from the logically prescribed answers.

Inductive inferences are not supported by formal logic because they do not conform to the principle of necessity. No matter how many times I see my pen fall to the ground when I drop it, I cannot infer that this is always the case as a matter of logical necessity. Historically, the illogical nature of inductive inference has caused much debate in the philosophy of science since scientific inferences themselves appear to be inductive, with general laws inferred from specific observations. This issue is discussed in Chapter Three, along with experiments which attempt to model scientific reasoning. In these studies subjects are required to discover rules and laws which govern an artificial universe of the experimenter's creation, to which end they must conduct their own "experiments". The major interest in this work concerns the soundness of the strategies used to formulate, test, and eliminate alternative hypotheses.

Apart from rule discovery, the other main form of inductive inference that has attracted psychological research is that of intuitive statistical inference. Most psychologists are familiar with at least some types of formal statistical inference such as the testing for statistical significance of experimental findings. Statistical inferences are traditionally described as relating one or more hypotheses (*H*) to some observation or datum (*D*). For example, a significance level is the conditional probability $P(D/Ho)$ where D is the experimental observation and Ho is the null hypothesis.

Mathematical statistics provides a normative theory for statistical inferences, in the same way that formal logic provides a criterion for assessing competence in deductive reasoning. For example, the law of large numbers states that a large sample of data will represent the characteristics of the underlying population with reasonable accuracy, whereas small samples may be very misleading. When people make statistical inferences intuitively, the question arises as to whether or not their judgements respect the law of large numbers (see Chapter Two for a discussion of the relevant literature). This is obviously an important issue in everyday inductive reasoning since one's willingness to generalise from experience should depend upon the adequacy of the sample of evidence experienced. It has been claimed that erroneous social inferences, leading for example to prejudice, arise because people are sensitive neither to the size nor the possible bias in samples from which they draw their conclusions (Nisbett & Ross, 1980). As with deductive reasoning, a large psychological literature exists reporting studies which ask people to make judgements about probabilities or draw inferences about uncertain situations with similarly widespread reporting of errors and biases.

Although the literatures on the different types of reasoning described are largely disjoint, examples of studies of deductive, inductive and statistical reasoning will be drawn upon in the course of this book. I have chosen to do this for several reasons. First of all, whilst the logical distinctions between the different forms of inference are reasonably clear, there is no reason to suppose that the organisation of human reasoning respects the boundaries laid down by philosophers. Similarly, the fact that the studies are reported in several distinct literatures which provide little cross-referencing to each other, again reflects only different traditions of psychological study. It is the history of psychological work, not the nature of people's reasoning which creates the division. Finally, I wish to draw my conclusions from the broadest possible knowledge base so as to maximise the chance of identifying general characteristics of human thinking and to minimise the risk of focusing on phenomena which are specific to particular experimental paradigms.

THE RATIONALITY DEBATE

Since the focus of this book is on bias and error in reasoning, I must address the question of how reasoning accuracy is measured and the controversy surrounding the issue of rationality in reasoning. A number of authors have objected that the numerous reports of error and bias in reasoning experiments are misleading and exaggerated and that people are a good deal more rational than they would appear to be from a casual reading of this literature. An important contribution was made, for example, by the philosopher L. Jonathan Cohen (1981) who argued that psychological experiments cannot be used to demonstrate irrationality. Obviously enough I do not accept this proposition, but a number of the arguments raised by Cohen and others are important and require careful consideration.

The first argument concerns the competence/performance distinction first proposed by Chomsky (1957; 1965) in the context of linguistic theory. Chomsky argued that the job of the linguist was to describe the underlying competence system of language which would always be subject to distortion through performance factors when language is used. For example, many spoken utterances are ungrammatical because the speaker forgets the earlier part of a long sentence and fails to make an appropriate completion of the structure. A number of authors have applied the distinction to reasoning so that mistakes may sometimes be attributed to performance factors rather than to defects in underlying logical competence.

The competence/performance distinction is useful in the context of reasoning theory, and I shall make some use of this terminology in this book. I should make it clear that the concern of this book is essentially with reasoning performance and the biases associated with it. I am not actually motivated by concern over the issue of whether humans are fundamentally rational or not. If people's reasoning performance is subject to error and bias then I want to know why this occurs and whether it can be corrected. It gives me no comfort, as it apparently does Cohen, to think that underneath it all may lie a true rational competence. What does interest me very much is understanding why apparent competence in logical and statistical reasoning exhibited under one set of circumstances is so frequently absent in others. A number of examples of this phenomenon will be discussed in the following chapters.

A second argument advanced by defenders of rationality rests upon another dichotomy: that between mental representations and processes. For example, Henle (1962), in an influential paper, argued that people's deductive reasoning follows the laws of logic and that apparent inferential errors reflect idiosyncratic representation of the problem content. In selective discussion of some protocols of syllogistic reasoning, she argued that subjects may add to, drop, or alter the premises given. In other words, the subject reasons not with the problem as given, but with a personalised representation of it. Relative to that representation, however, the reasoning is logical. This theory has been developed by other psychologists as, for example, in the Revlis (1975a; 1975b) "conversion" theory of syllogistic reasoning.

Clearly, the representation/process distinction is an important one, though a curious defence of rationality. Is it rational for subjects to ignore the instructions, distort the information given, and bring in extraneous beliefs? I do, however, agree that reasoning biases often arise in the course of representing the problem information, a central assumption of the theory proposed by Evans (1984a) and developed in the course of this book. This is not, however, to say that the subsequent process of reasoning is necessarily logical and indeed I have argued in an earlier detailed discussion of deductive reasoning that the Henle hypothesis is unsound in this regard (see Evans, 1982). A number of biases observed in conditional reasoning, for example, would not appear to be consistent with logical reasoning, no matter how the conditional is represented.

A third objection is that experimental tasks used by psychologists may be arbitrary, artificial, confusing, and generally unrepresentative of real life reasoning (see Cohen, 1981; Berkeley & Humphreys, 1982; Beach, Christensen-Szalanski, & Barnes, 1987; and Kahneman & Tversky, 1982a). This reveals a general dilemma in experimental psychology: the trade-off between control and realism. It is very hard to understand psychological processes in the field without experimental manipulations, but controlled laboratory studies are always open to criticisms on the grounds of artificiality. There does seem to be a genuine problem here in that observed reasoning performance can be quite drastically affected by changes in the presentation of the task or the framing of the instructions. This is well illustrated, for example, in the study of people's understanding of the law of large numbers (see Chapter Two). However, careful examination of these effects can be revealing about the nature of the factors responsible for affecting performance and there is no *a priori* reason to assume that such factors will not be operative also, outside of the laboratory. Certainly, the widespread assumption of authors such as Cohen (1981) that merely framing problems in more realistic terms enhances performance is now known to be oversimplified. Variations in problem content can, in fact, have both biasing and debiasing effects as will be discussed in detail in Chapter Four. It is certainly not the case that reasoning competence is simply suppressed by artificiality and released by realism, as we shall see.

A further argument of rationalist authors is that there is a citation bias in the literature (Christensen-Szalanski & Beach, 1984). The claim is that papers which report good reasoning are cited far less frequently than those reporting errors and biases. The study was based upon statistical rather than deductive reasoning. Having conducted a detailed survey of the latter field (cf. Evans, 1982), I must comment that very few studies reporting error-free reasoning have actually been published for tasks involving syllogistic or propositional logic, and that the errors reported have proved highly replicable. However, even accepting the evidence within the domain studied by Christensen-Szalanski and Beach, the citation bias can be defended on the grounds that studying erroneous reasoning is generally more interesting and more informative about underlying processes (see Evans, 1984b). It should be noted that Berkeley and Humphreys (1982) have also turned the attack on to the authors of papers reporting bias, claiming that it is often psychologists' explanations rather than subjects' reasoning which is at fault and implying, as do Christensen-Szalanski and Beach, that it is a matter of fashion to attribute biases to experimental subjects.

Perhaps the most telling argument to arise from proponents of rationality (e.g. Cohen, 1979; 1981; 1982) is that reports of error are relative to the normative system assumed by the experimenter. Many authors take a system such as standard propositional logic or Bayesian decision theory as an absolute standard of correctness and lament any departure of their subjects' behaviour from its prescriptions. Cohen and others have pointed out that the subject may be reasoning quite rationally according to some alternative system of logic or probability. Psychologists are perhaps insufficiently aware of the range of alternatives to standard logics which are discussed in the philosophical literature.

Despite the emphasis on bias in my own work, I actually have a long-standing sympathy for the argument about standard logics. I have, for example, advocated for a long time that deductive reasoning performance should be reported in terms of what inferences were and were not made and not in terms of right and wrong (see Evans, 1972a). I still, however, believe that it is possible to identify clear evidence of bias in many cases. In essence, I define an error as failure to make an inference that *any* reasonable normative theory would classify as necessary, or endorsement of a similarly universally recognised fallacy. A *bias*, which may account for such errors, is a systematic tendency to take account of factors irrelevant to the task at hand or to ignore relevant factors. Relevance is again defined on as broad and uncontroversial a basis as possible.

For example, the law of large numbers is not simply a feature of standard statistical theory, it is a phenomenon readily demonstrated by empirical means such as a computer simulation. Hence, I am quite happy to say that intuitive statistical judgements which take no account of sample size are in error. Unlike many other authors in the deductive reasoning literature, however, I have never described conditional inferences as "errors" simply because they were consistent with an equivalence interpretation of *If p then q* (i.e., one in which q is also taken to imply p) whereas standard logic text books use this to denote implication. The logical rule of material implication is in fact an abstract notion that is only mapped for convenience on to the conditional sentence; the equivalence relationship is a perfectly plausible alternative for a natural language user to adopt in some contexts. I would, however, describe failure to make *Modus Tollens* as erroneous as well as the usual behaviour observed on Wason's selection task (described in Chapter Two). In these cases there is no plausible interpretation of the statement which would not entail the inference concerned.

Although there are arguments arising in the rationality debate which are relevant to our purposes, the central issue in many ways is not. It is not my purpose to demonstrate the fundamentally irrational nature of human beings nor to argue about the merits and demerits of alternative systems of logic. There is, in my view, sufficient evidence of widespread mistakes and biases in human reasoning—on very robust criteria of measurement—to justify a systematic attempt to classify such phenomena and consider both the theoretical origins and practical implications of such findings. I see this effort as complementary to, rather than in opposition to the efforts of other psychologists to propose mechanisms underlying the competence which is also manifest in reasoning studies. A brief review of these approaches is now required.

THEORIES OF REASONING

In a previous work I presented a detailed and eclectic review of psychological reasearch on deductive reasoning conducted up until around 1980 (Evans, 1982). Whilst I argued that many examples of systematic biases were manifest in the studies reviewed, I also pointed out that almost all the paradigms studied provided evidence of logical competence also. In other words, most deductive reasoning experiments show that subjects' responses are systematically influenced by the logical structure of the problems whilst *at the same time* often biased also by logically irrelevant features of the problems. A good example is provided by the study of belief bias in syllogistic reasoning by Evans, Barston, and Pollard (1983, as discussed in detail in Chapter Four) who found that validity judgements were strongly influenced both by the actual logical validity of the syllogisms and by the (logically irrelevant) prior believability of the conclusions. Thus there is both a logical and a non-logical component of reasoning performance to be explained.

One possible approach to explaining such findings is to propose that there are parallel and competing influences of a logical and non-logical nature—the explanation favoured in the Evans (1982) review. The "logical" component in this scheme referred to a presumed process of reasoning sensitive to the logic of the problems, but without assumption about the nature of this process. An alternative—and perhaps more popular—approach is to define a competence theory of reasoning and then to specify cognitive constraints that will explain the presence of errors and biases in observed performance. Whilst the present book is primarily concerned with the understanding of the factors responsible for biases, a brief examination of the main approaches to explanation of competence and performance in reasoning is needed to place the discussion in the context of contemporary reasoning theory. For more detailed discussion and evaluation of such theories see Evans (1987b; in press).

Theories of Deductive Reasoning

Considering first the case of deductive reasoning, there are essentially three main classes of theory which identify reasoning competence respectively with utilisation of (a) general purpose inference rules, (b) domain or context sensitive rules and (c) mental models. The first approach assumes that people possess what Johnson-Laird (1983) calls a "mental logic". A number of psychologists have traditionally proposed that standard formal logic describes—as well as prescribes—the nature of human reasoning (e.g., Inhelder & Piaget, 1958; Henle, 1962). Recent authors have favoured the use of natural logics in which an explicit set of elementary inference rules or schemas are defined as the building blocks of human deductive inference (e.g., Braine, 1978; Rips, 1983). Hence, human reasoning is seen as akin to a proof in formal logic in which rules are applied to combinations of premises in order to generate intermediate and final conclusions.

These theories are essentially *syntactic* in that they apply to the form of a sentence without regard to its content or meaning. The only means by which the well-documented effects of semantic factors on reasoning can be explained is in the process of translating problem content into the abstract representations to which inference shcemata are applied and by the conversion of inferences back into the real world domain. However, inference rules theorists have to date made little attempt to specify the processes involved which would have to be very complex indeed (see Chapter Four and Evans, in press, for further discussion of this point). A further weakness in the approach generally is that little attempt has been made to specify a model of the cognitive processes which would be required actually to apply inference rules to make deductions. The notable exception is to be found in Rips (1983) who develops a process model, implemented as a working computer program, to tackle this precise problem.

A second approach meets the problem of content effects head on by proposing that people possess content specific or at least domain sensitive rules. In this approach the rules applied to a given problem will depend upon the meaning and context of the premises and hence can explain why people's reasoning is not simply a reflection of the logical structure of the problems. The most promising approach of this type assumes that knowledge is organised in units called "schemas" which are retrieved from memory and "fitted" to the features of the current problem (see e.g., Rumelhart, 1980; Cheng & Holyoak, 1985). Such schemas may include rules for reasoning and action appropriate to a general type of problem which has been identified. The applicability of schema theories to the explanation of content effects in reasoning is examined in Chapter Four.

Schema theory can explain "competence" in so far as the rules of a given schema are isomorphic with those of formal logic and performance "errors" due to the use of schemas whose rules diverge from those of logic. However, it is not apparent at present how such theories can explain either the evidence of logical competence or the biases from *syntactic* factors, such as negation, which are a feature of many studies of reasoning with arbitrary problem content (see Evans, 1982). A theory which claims to provide an account of competence and performance with either artificial or semantically rich problem content is that of reasoning with mental models (Johnson-Laird, 1983).

The mental models theory proposes that logically competent reasoning can be achieved without any use of rules, either generally purpose of domain specific. It is proposed that what people do when they reason is to attempt to test whether a conclusion must be true given that its premises are true. In order to achieve this, it is proposed that on reading the premises of a problem, the subject constructs mental models to represent possible states of the world consistent with the information given. These models include concrete tokens to represent different classes of objects and are structurally isomorphic with the world situation being modelled. A provisional deduction is formed on the basis of any proposition which is clearly true in the model but not directly stated in the premises. In order to ensure validity, however, subjects are assumed to search for counter-examples by attempting to construct alternative models in which the premises are also true but in which the conclusion may not hold. Where no such counter-example is found the inference is declared valid.

Mental models theory can account for logical competence with arbitrary problem content, since subjects are assumed to understand the truth conditions of a connective (e.g., if . . . then) or quantifier (e.g., some, all). However, content effects can also be explained on the grounds that certain models will be suggested or inhibited according to prior knowledge about the situation described. Two main types of performance factor have also been proposed in this line of work. Firstly, subjects are assumed to have limited working memory capacity such that the more models required to evaluate the inference the more likely they are to make a mistake (Johnson-Laird & Bara, 1984). Secondly, belief bias effects may operate since subjects may lack the motivation to seek counter-examples when a congenial conclusion can be found which is consistent with the premises (Oakhill & Johnson-Laird, 1985b).

Theories of Statistical Reasoning

Statistical inference is normally interpreted within a framework known as *behavioural decision theory*—a somewhat ambiguous term applied to both prescriptive and descriptive approaches. The origins of the prescriptive theory arise from two main sources. The first is in game theory, a systematic description of how a "rational man" should make decisions under different conditions, e.g. uncertainty or rational competition (Von Neumann & Morgenstern, 1947). The basic tenets of this approach are that a decision tree is constructed to project the consequences of alternative actions in terms of both probabilities and utilities (subjective values of pay-offs). Decision makers are then assumed to make choices according to a decision rule—typically that of maximising expected utility. Since most real life decisions are made under uncertainty, application of the theory has required a systematic approach to probability and statistical hypothesis testing. The approach favoured has been Bayesian decision theory which differs from conventional inferential statistics based on null hypothesis testing in two important respects. Firstly, a subjective rather than frequentist theory of probability is assumed—hence a probability is simply a number between zero and one which represents the degree of confidence or belief that an individual holds about the occurrence of an event. Secondly, the theory holds that one cannot sensibly discuss the likelihood of an hypothesis in isolation, but must consider the relative probability of two or more competitors.

The normative decision theory derived from this background has been applied for some years in a practice known as *decision analysis*. Psychologists have been much involved in this activity which is based upon helping decision makers to structure their problems in a systematic manner which allows a decision-theoretic solution to be formulated (see von Winterfeldt & Edwards, 1986). Decision analysis will be discussed in the final chapter of this book with respect to the problem of debiasing. Our concern here, however, is more with descriptive behaviour decision theory. At one time, it was thought that the normative theory provided an adequate basis for a descriptive theory, i.e. that man was a good Bayesian decision maker (Peterson & Beach, 1967). As with Henle's (1962) optimistic view of logic as a performance theory of deductive reasoning, however, this idea was not held up in the light of the results of the many psychological experiments conducted subsequently (see, for example, Slovic, Fischhoff, & Lichtenstein, 1977).

Since the early 1970s, work on statistical inference has been dominated by the theoretical papers of Daniel Kahneman and Amos Tversky, the leading proponents of the so-called "heuristics and biases" approach (see Kahneman, Slovic, & Tversky, 1982). The theory proposes that people make statistical inferences and judgements by the use of heuristics such as "representativeness" and "availability" (to be described in Chapter Two). In their use of the term, a heuristic is a short-cut and essentially simple "rule of thumb" in contrast with the complex workings of normative decision theory which would be very hard to apply intuitively. In a series of papers, Kahneman and Tversky sought to show that while such heuristics may be appropriate in some contexts, they result in a large range of errors and biases on many experimental tasks requiring intuitive statistical inferences, and have claimed that such biases are likely to be prevalent in real life and expert decision making (cf. Kahneman, Slovic, & Tversky, 1982).

The competence/performance distinction is not as clearly utilised in theories of statistical reasoning as it is in the case of deduction. However, Kahneman and Tversky (1982a) modified their position somewhat in the light of evidence that many of the biases reported in their own experiments were shown subsequently to be dependent upon problem presentation, and that reasoning competence may have been underestimated. In this paper, Kahneman and Tversky suggested that subjects may hold normatively appropriate "rules"—such as the law of large numbers—as well as heuristics. They emphasise, however, that possession of a rule does not mean that it will necessarily be correctly applied.

APPROACH AND FORM OF THIS BOOK

The previous section has given a brief survey of contemporary approaches to theories of both deductive and statistical reasoning. There is a certain amount of cross-fertilisation between the two areas so that for example Pollard (1982) has applied the availability heuristic to the explanation of deductive reasoning performance, whilst some decision researchers are applying the concept of mental models and scenario generation to the forecasting of future events (e.g., Kahneman & Tversky, 1982b; Jungermann & Thuring, 1987). Such developments are most welcome since, as already stated, it is assumed here that similar psychological processes are involved in the different types of inference.

As already indicated, this book is concerned with the explanation of biases in reasoning and does not attempt to present a theory of reasoning processes as such. However, since biases account for a substantial portion of the behaviour observed in studies of human reasoning it does form a theoretical account of many of the phenomena and one which complements the efforts of those psychologists—discussed in the previous section—who are concerned with reasoning mechanisms *per se*. To put it another way, the emphasis here is upon the understanding of performance constraints rather than upon a theory of reasoning competence.

The theoretical stance taken in this book is based upon a development of earlier discussions provided by Evans (1983a; 1984a). This framework, which is described in more detail in Chapter Two, assumes that biases in reasoning tasks of all kinds are principally attributable to selective processing of the problem information. Such selection frequently takes place in what Evans (1984a) calls the *heuristic* stage of reasoning, responsible for representing the psychologically "relevant" features of the problem. Errors of omission or commission in these relevance judgements will bias the outcome of subsequent reasoning, no matter how soundly based it may be in itself. The *analytic* reasoning which is applied to the representation of the problem provides the basis for observed logical competence, though it may well be subject to further selective processing and other performance factors.

I have not previously, not will I here, commit myself to a definite view on the mechanism by which analytic reasoning is achieved. Nearly 20 years study of human reasoning have not been sufficient for me to form a clear conclusion on this matter. However, I will say that I find the theory of reasoning based upon general inference rules particularly unconvincing for a number of reasons, especially relating to the effects of content variables (see Evans, in press and Chapter Four of this book). In so far as the "heuristics" proposed by Kahneman and Tversky are also formulated as very general principles applicable to many diverse situations, I hold similar reservations about this approach also. Of the remaining alternatives, I am attracted both by the theory of pragmatic reasoning schemas and by that of mental models despite their apparent incompatibility. Each theory is applied very convincingly to the explanation of a number of experimental findings, but each is also hard to apply to a range of other well-established phenomena, and neither has received experimental evaluation over a large range of tasks. At present—for me at least—there is no clear singular solution to the problem of reasoning competence.

In spite of this shocking admission of ignorance, I will endeavour to provide in this book a consistent and coherent theoretical explanation of biases in human reasoning as well as a discussion of their implications. The main review and discussion of theory and research which follows in Chapters Two to Five is of necessity selective, drawing as it does on several large and diverse literatures. Chapter content is organised not by the type of reasoning paradigm studied but by the issue addressed, with illustrative material from different literatures included as appropriate.

In Chapter Two, I focus on the basic notion of selective processing as a cause of bias. First of all, a number of theoretical ideas relevant to this notion are examined including availability, vividness, relevance, and working memory capacity. Then empirical case studies drawn from the literatures on deductive and statistical reasoning are considered in turn. The first of these involves a persistent selective processing bias in conditional reasoning, whereas the second review looks at the influence of sample size in intuitive statistical inference. These case studies are revealing of a number of general facets of reasoning research.

Chapter Three addresses the topic of "confirmation bias"—claimed by many to be one of the best supported and most important biases shown in the reasoning literature. Several experimental literatures are relevant to this claim and are examined in some detail in the chapter. However, an alternative explanation of the phenomena is offered to that which dominates in the literature. Specifically, it is proposed that errors on these tasks reflect a selective processing bias based upon a preference for positive over negative information and do not necessarily indicate any motivational tendency for subjects to try to confirm their own theories as is commonly believed.

Chapter Four concerns perhaps the most important issue in experimental research on reasoning—the influence which the content of reasoning problems, as opposed to their formal structure, has on the inferences drawn. The chapter examines both biasing and debiasing effects of problem content. With respect to the former, attention is concentrated on the belief bias effect and a theoretical explanation advanced which falls directly within the Evans (1984a) heuristic/analytic framework. The second part of the chapter deals with the widespread, but dubious, belief that logical reasoning is generally facilitated by problem content. It is argued that facilitation of reasoning occurs only when people have learned methods of reasoning in real life domains analogous to the problem content and which have a functional correspondence to the outcome of a logical analysis.

The topic of self-knowledge in reasoning is dealt with in Chapter Five because it is particularly relevant to the present theory of biases and to the problem of debiasing. The theoretical approach taken in this book assumes that the representational heuristics responsible for many biases constitute preconscious processes. Subjects are aware of that to which they are attending but not of the selective process directing their attention. If biases occur at an unconscious and non-verbal level then it is likely that people will not be aware of their operation and that verbal instruction may not be a useful approach to debiasing. The literatures discussed in this chapter include studies of explicit and implicit thought processes in control tasks, accuracy of confidence in intuitive judgements and the nature of verbal reports of reasoning strategies, all of which point to severe limitations in people's knowledge of their own thought processes. The theoretical issues arising are discussed in the context of recent significant papers in the psychological literature.

Finally, Chapter Six is concerned with the practical implications of the issues discussed in the book and addresses the problem of debiasing—that is, how best to reduce the presence of bias in human reasoning and to minimise its impact on real life decision making. Particular attention is given to the possibilities of improving reasoning by education and training and to minimising the effects of bias by the development of interactive decision aids.

2 Selective Processing

As I will argue throughout this book, the major cause of bias in human reasoning and judgement lies in factors which induce people to process the problem information in a selective manner. Such selection may arise either in the process of forming mental representations of the information presented in the problem or else in the actual manner in which it is subsequently processed. For example, if the reasoner fails—for whatever reason—to attend to some logically relevant aspect of the problem then no amount of good subsequent reasoning is likely to lead to a correct solution. Equally, a common cause of bias is that people often attend to—and take account of—logically *irrelevant* features of the problem.

The notion that selective processing may lead to error in thinking and problem solving has quite a long history, and was especially emphasised by the pre-war school of Gestalt psychology. One of the important ideas arising here was that of mental "sets", in which it proposed that reinforcement of a particular problem-solving method may lead to rigid application of the strategy to new problems. Such sets may have positive or negative effects: for example, if a series of anagrams can be solved by rearranging the letters in the same order then this will facilitate the solution to new anagrams of the same type, but inhibit solution of those requiring a different rearrangement of letters. Similarly, Duncker (1945) proposed the idea of "functional fixity" to explain why people find it hard to think of using objects in novel ways to solve problems, once the function of the object has been fixed by knowledge of its normal use.

The Gestalt psychologists generally treated the notion of set in a very negative manner, emphasising the consequent loss of flexibility and creativity in human thinking (e.g., Luchins & Luchins, 1950). Although I shall also, in the course of this book, frequently refer to selective processing as a cause of error and bias in reasoning I would not wish to convey the impression that selectivity in thinking is unintelligent. On the contrary, in thinking—as in perception—the brain is faced with a massive information reduction problem and any attempt to process all available information would obviously be impossible. Indeed, some authors—such as Newell and Simon (1972) in their important studies of human problem solving—have described the role of selective reduction of the search space, by application of appropriate heuristics, almost as the defining characteristic of intelligent behaviour.

The paradoxical nature of the above comments is more apparent than real. The cognitive processes by which we make sense of the world around us are in essence and necessarily of a selective nature. Selection *is* fundamental to intelligence. However, mistakes in selection inevitably occur and when these are systematic they may lead to an observed bias in inferential behaviour. Our concern must then be (a) to understand the nature of selective mechanisms in cognitive processing and (b) to identify the conditions under which such mechanisms will lead to errors and biases. One of the simpler notions here is that of limited cognitive capacity, that is the accepted view that people can only attend to—or hold in working memory—a limited amount of information at one time, such that overload will lead to errors. A deeper level of explanation involves consideration of the mechanisms responsible for selecting information and their interaction with the features of the problem itself. Hence, we may ask what it is that makes some items appear more salient, vivid or relevant than others?

This chapter is divided into two main sections. In the first, I shall look at several related theoretical concepts that concern selective processing in human inference, namely availability, relevance, vividness, and working memory capacity. In the second section, I shall present two empirical case studies of reasoning biases—one drawn from the literature on deductive reasoning and the other from the literature on statistical inference. In each case, it will be argued that the results of experimental studies of these biases can best be explained by selective processing of the problem information.

THEORETICAL CONCEPTS

Availability

The notion of "availability" refers simply to information which is actually attended to or thought about by the subject when performing some cognitive task. Although related notions such as perceptual salience as determinants of attention, or priming effects in learning tasks have been around for much longer, current interest in the application of the idea of availability in the field of inference stems from the paper of Tversky and Kahneman (1973).

This is one of the series of highly influential papers on the "heuristics and biases" approach to probabilistic inference and judgement by this pair of authors which date from the early 1970s up to the present time. The general theoretical stance they propose is that intuitive assessments of probability bear scant attention to the dictates of probability theory, but instead reflect the usage of fairly simple heuristics—the best known of which are "representativeness" (discussed later in the chapter) and "availability". These heuristics, however, often lead to systematic errors and biases, leading to the common description of this whole line of work as the "heuristics and biases" approach.

The original use of the term "availability" by Tversky and Kahneman (1973) was quite specific and limited to the domain of intuitive probability judgements. They proposed that: "A person is said to employ the availability heuristic whenever he estimates frequency or probability by the ease with which instances or associations could be brought to mind." On the face of it, this sounds like a quite reasonable method for estimating probabilities and one which is quite likely to lead to correct answers. For example, a doctor examining a patient might recall a number of case histories of patients presenting similar symptoms in her past experience, and use this information to estimate the likelihood of rival diagnoses in the present case. Provided that the doctor's memory is accurate and that her experience encompasses a sufficiently large and unbiased sample of exemplars, this should provide a fairly accurate guide to probability.

Why, then, should use of the availability heuristic produce biases in intuitive probability judgements? One of the main reasons to be demonstrated in the various experiments of Tversky and Kahneman is that of cognitive constraints, for example in the organisation and retrieval methods associated with human memory. In one experiment they showed that people judge words with k as the initial letter to occur more frequently in the English language than those with k as the third letter. Objectively the answer is wrong. The problem is not that people do not know more words with k in the third position, but rather that retrieval by initial letters is much easier, enabling more such words to be "brought to mind". In another experiment, subjects were read a list of names and asked to judge whether more were male or female. The lists were so constructed that either male names were of famous people and female names of unknown people or vice versa. In either case, the great majority of subjects judged the famous names to be more numerous although they were actually in the minority. In this case, selective storage of the more memorable names would appear to underlie the bias.

Tversky and Kahneman also demonstrated that availability biases could be triggered by expectancies and prior beliefs, by reference to the phenomenon of "illusory correlation" originally demonstrated by Chapman and Chapman (1967; 1969). The Chapmans' work showed, for example, that clinicians provided with a series of case descriptions will perceive patterns of relations between clinical tests and diagnoses which conform with their prior beliefs, but are not actually present in the data presented. Tversky and Kahneman (1973) provide some supporting evidence of the "illusory correlation" effect in one of their own experiments. In this case the bias arises from selective encoding and retrieval of evidence which favours a prior belief and could thus lead to maintenance of false theories—a phenomenon related to the confirmation and belief bias effects to be discussed in later chapters of this book.

Availability biases can also arise from accurate recall of a biased set of exemplars. For example, it has been shown by Lichtenstein, Slovic, Fischhoff, and Layman (1978) that people radically overestimate the likelihood of dying from accidents as compared with illnesses. The availability explanation of this is that the media provide highly selective coverage of violent and spectacular accidents (e.g., airplane crashes) but very little coverage of deaths by routine causes such as strokes and heart attacks unless the individual is famous. There seems little doubt that media coverage does engender heavily distorted perceptions of risk. For example, many people are deterred from visiting Northern Ireland on the grounds of the highly publicised terrorism though they are actually more likely to be killed there in a traffic accident.

The Tversky and Kahneman paper is not only important in terms of its original objective of explaining a major cause of bias in probability judgements, but also for wider reasons. It is useful to distinguish between the determinants of availability of information and usage that is made of that information. The point is that the kinds of biases in memory retrieval that they identify could influence tasks other than probability judgements. Many judgements or inferences can be affected by information "called to mind". For example, a courtroom jury needs to weigh evidence for and against the defendant. If the memorial availability is affected by psychological factors—e.g. primacy and recency effects, "vividness" of different types of evidence (discussed later), and so on—then the judgement could be biased accordingly.

Pollard (1982) specifically attempted to widen the scope of the availability concept and apply it to a range of phenomena in deductive and inductive reasoning tasks which do not involve judgements of probability. Although he frequently refers to the availability "heuristic" this often cannot be taken literally in terms of the original Tversky and Kahneman definition when frequency judgements are not involved. He seems rather to be arguing that responses in reasoning tasks—for example, selecting an item, generating an hypothesis, or evaluating a conclusion—are mediated "directly" by available cues rather than any process of reasoning *per se*. The flavour of Pollard's arguments can be illustrated by reference to one of the phenomena he discusses—belief bias in deductive reasoning (see Chapter Four for detailed discussion of this effect).

The belief bias effect arises when subjects evaluate the validity of an argument on the basis of whether or not its conclusions conform to their prior beliefs, rather than on the basis of whether it is logically entailed by the premises. Pollard comments: "Truth status can only be assessed on the basis of what the subject can *retrieve* from his experience or, in Tversky and Kahneman terms, on the basis of the availability of relevant information...It is also possible that the availability of the conclusion directly mediates evaluation of both truth status *and* validity." He later attempts to justify this non-reasoning as follows: "Direct evaluation of evidence is...an advantageous real life behaviour...The essential difference between experimental and real life situations is that, in the latter, logical validity is not the salient dimension and it matters not at all whether an invalid conclusion, or inference, is accepted as long as it is *true*, or whether a valid conclusion is rejected, as long as it is *false*."

Pollard appears to be arguing that memory retrieval is more effective than reasoning in solving problems and that behaviour only appears biased because it is viewed within the context of an artificial laboratory task. Whilst I accept many of his arguments on the biasing effects of memorial availability, I cannot agree with this overall conclusion. Manifestly people do *need* to reason in real life, and equally obviously they do *succeed* in reasoning—at least to an extent—in the laboratory. Staying with the belief bias effect as an example, whilst Evans, Barston, and Pollard (1983) demonstrated the presence of extensive belief bias in subjects' evaluations of syllogistic arguments they also found equally strong effects of the logical validity of the premises. More generally, in my earlier extensive review of laboratory based deductive reasoning tasks (Evans, 1982), I concluded that most such studies show a mixture of logical and non-logical effects.

In essence, then, the notion that available information, i.e. that easily "brought to mind", may bias behaviour on reasoning tasks of all kinds—and not simply probability judgements—is acceptable, though the idea that memory retrieval can and does replace reasoning processes is not. However, even the "availability" notion itself is perhaps too simple as we shall see in the following section.

Relevance

There is a fundamental problem with the generalised availability hypothesis. The negative side is all right—people will err if logically pertinent information is not available or heeded. However, it is not the case that simply making relevant information available will ensure that it is taken into account. A clear example of this is provided by experiments on the "base rate fallacy"—a phenomenon first described by Kahneman and Tversky (1972a;

1973) and which has attracted much interest in the subsequent psychological literature.

Perhaps the best known example discussed in the literature is the "cabs" problem (Kahneman & Tversky, 1972a). Subjects are told that two cab companies run in a city: the Blue cab company which has 85% of the city's cabs, and the Green cab company which has 15%. A cab is involved in a hit and run accident and a witness later identified the cab as a Green one. Under tests the witness was shown to be able to identify the colour of a cab correctly about 80% of the time under similar viewing conditions, but would confuse it with the other colour about 20% of the time. The subjects are then asked whether it is more likely that the cab is, in fact, a Green or Blue one. Most subjects say Green though the correct answer is, in fact, Blue.

The solution can be demonstrated by an application of Bayes' theorem which provides an equation for estimating the posterior odds between two rival hypotheses—that is to say their relative likelihood after examining a piece of relevant evidence. In this case the alternative hypotheses are Blue and Green cab and the evidence is the testimony of the witness. Bayes' theorem states that the posterior odds are a product of the ratio of the prior odds (or base rates) and the likelihood ratio. The prior odds are clearly 85 to 15 in favour of the Blue hypothesis. The likelihood ratio refers to the relative likelihood that the evidence (witness says Green) could have arisen given each hypothesis. The chance is 20% given a Blue cab and 80% given a Green one: hence yielding a likelihood ratio of 20 to 80 in favour of Green. However, the product of these two ratios yields posterior odds of 17 to 12 in favour of the *Blue* cab.

Numerous experiments involving the cabs problem and other tasks have shown generally that subjects' probability judgements will ignore or severely neglect base rate information provided that any specific evidence is presented, even if that evidence is totally *non-diagnostic*, i.e. fails to discriminate the hypotheses under consideration at all. This presents particular difficulties for the generalised availability hypothesis of Pollard (1982) since a feature of these tasks is that the base rate data are made highly salient in the problem presentations. Indeed, one might reasonably argue that its presentation involves "demand characteristics" cueing subjects that it is relevant to the answer—and yet they ignore it.

Bar-Hillel (1980) has argued that base rate data are ignored because people fail to perceive their *relevance*. One determinant of perceived relevance demonstrated in the literature is the elicitation of a causal schema (e.g., Ajzen, 1977; Tversky & Kahneman, 1980). For example, performance on the cabs problem is greatly improved if subjects are told that there are equal numbers of Blue and Green cabs but that 85% of the cabs *involved in accidents* are Blue ones. The image of reckless Blue cab drivers conjured up by this information apparently provides subjects with a causal connection between Blue cabs and accidents which facilitates utilisation of the base rate data (the problem is, of course, statistically equivalent). Bar-Hillel (1980) argues, with experimental evidence, that causality is only one factor which might cue the relevance of the usually neglected information.

The "relevance" concept lies at the heart of a recent theoretical paper in which I distinguish between *heuristic* and *analytic* processes in reasoning (Evans, 1984a). My use of the term "heuristic" differs somewhat from that of Kahneman and Tversky and so needs careful definition. The theory essentially proposes that reasoning proceeds in two stages: (1) a heuristic stage in which aspects of the problem information are identified as "relevant" and selected for further processing; and (2) an analytic stage in which inferences are drawn from the selected information (see Fig. 2.1). The function of the heuristic stage is to identify psychologically relevant aspects of the information given and also to retrieve associated relevant information from memory. The heuristic processes are considered to be entirely unconscious because they are *pre-attentive*, i.e. they determine what subjects will attend to and think about.

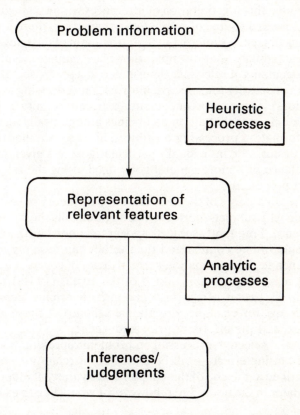

FIG. 2.1.   The two-stage reasoning process (from Evans, 1984).

The potential confusion of terminology here arises since Kahneman and Tversky's use of the term "heuristics" refers to methods of drawing inferences and are hence one of the rival candidates—together, for example, with schemas and mental models—for explaining what I term the "analytic" stage. What I am really referring to are *representational* heuristics which are preconscious determinants of the subject's representation of the problem information. A good example is provided by the way in which chess players immediately "see" that just a few of the many legal moves in a given board position (and a similar subset of possible replies) are worth analysing. Most other reasoning theories are concerned with describing the processes involved in drawing inferences from mental representations rather than those involved in forming them. However, the point of the paper was to argue that we cannot understand *how* people reason, until we know what they are reasoning *about*.

A recent theory of verbal communication presented by Sperber and Wilson (1986) is also based on the concept of relevance. Although they address different phenomena, principally the ways in which prior knowledge and belief determine the interpretation of utterances within context, and discuss relevance more as a source of competence than error, there is nevertheless an interesting degree of similarity in their treatment of the relevance concept to that presented here. For example, they place emphasis on the notion of intuitive judgements of relevance determined in a preconscious manner and also stress the necessity for selective information processing as the underlying reason for relevance as a fundamental aspect of cognition. For example (p. 49): "Our claim is that all human beings automatically aim at the most efficient information processing possible. This is so whether they are conscious of it or not... an individual's particular goal at a given moment is always an instance of a more general goal: maximising the relevance of the information processed."

One of the advantages of the heuristic/analytic theory of reasoning is that it can explain why subjects' performance so often falls short of their reasoning competence. Frequently subjects appear to understand a logical or statistical principle in one context and then totally fail to apply it in another. Failure to encode the information correctly can, of course, ensure that any subsequent reasoning will fail. Much of the Evans (1984a) paper is concerned with discussion of the factors which determine perceived relevance—including, for example, attentional salience of presentations, linguistic factors, and the effects of prior knowledge.

The causes of selective processing in problem representation—and their consequent biasing effects—will be discussed in relation to both the case studies described at the end of this chapter and a variety of other phenomena considered later in the book. First, however, I would like to examine briefly two further concepts relevant to the idea of selective information processing in human reasoning: vividness effects and working memory capacity.

Vividness

The concept of "vividness" as a cause of selective processing of information has been discussed in the literature on cognitive social psychology. Nisbett and Ross (1980) proposed the notion as an explanation of differential weighting given by people to evidence in social judgements, frequently resulting in biases. For example, an individual choosing a make of car to buy might be influenced more by the anecdotes of a close friend who ran a similar model, than by the much more probative evidence of a consumer survey report. Similarly, courtroom juries may be heavily influenced by the dramatic—though notoriously unreliable—evidence of eye-witnesses and relatively unimpressed by the dull meticulous testimony of expert forensic scientists.

In order to explain such apparent biases, Nisbett and Ross propose that subjects overweight vivid, concrete information and underweight dull, pallid, and abstract information. Specifically, they suggested that vividness of evidence is determined by: (1) emotional interest; (2) concreteness and imageability; and (3) temporal and spatial proximity. It is no coincidence that these factors—concreteness, recency, etc.—are also shown in the cognitive psychological literature to be associated with greater memorability. Indeed, the greater memorial availability of information is one of the main mechanisms by which Nisbett and Ross suppose that the vividness of information creates its disproportionate impact.

Whilst intuitively appealing, it must be recorded that the empirical basis for the vividness effect in social psychological studies has been strongly disputed by Taylor and Thompson (1982). The latter authors review a large range of attitude-change studies which manipulate factors which should affect vividness of information, and claim that the evidence for the predicted effects is very weak. They do, however, draw a distinction between vividness and *salience* studies, arguing that the latter effect is well supported by the evidence. The distinction they make is that salience studies specifically ensure that differential attention will be paid to the features concerned whereas vividness studies do not.

Clearly, the notions of vividness and salience are related to those of availability and relevance previously discussed. Information which is made salient by its means of presentation is more "available" to the subject. Similarly, the "vividness" of evidence—if indeed such a factor does operate—is a possible mechanism for influencing not only availability but perhaps perceived relevance as well. Detailed examination of issues in the social psychological literature is beyond the scope of this book. It is sufficient for our purposes to note the relevance of these concepts and bear them in mind in the discussion of possible causes of bias in human reasoning.

Working Memory Capacity

The discussion to date has focused on the question of why it is that an individual comes to be thinking about some aspect of a problem or some associated evidence retrieved from memory. It has been suggested that a variety of factors such as memory organisation, perceptual salience, causal schemas, linguistic cues, concreteness, etc. may play a role in the selective encoding of problems with its consequent effects on the inferences drawn. In addition to such factors we must also recognise that the attention span and working memory of humans is of severely limited capacity and that this in itself enforces selective processing of information.

The distinction between short-term memory (STM) and long-term memory (LTM) is, of course, well established in cognitive psychology. Generally, STM is considered to hold a small amount of recently attended information which is lost rapidly unless transferred into the more durable and far greater capacity storage of the LTM system. STM can be thought of as a moving window over our experiences—the container for the stream of consciousness, if you like. The question of what actually gets represented in, and is retrievable from, STM is important in the discussion of verbalisable knowledge and will be considered in detail in Chapter Five. For the present, the interest is in the notion that this STM functions as a *working memory*, and that its limited capacity severely constrains various cognitive processes including those responsible for reasoning.

The characterisation of STM as a working memory is important, since it implies that the store does more than simply act as a buffer between perception and LTM. Many cognitive processes require concurrent attention to several pieces of information. A good example is reading, in which attention must span a number of words in order for the reader to extract their syntactic relationship and parse the sentence. It is equally evident that reasoning processes should be affected by working memory capacity. For example, deductive reasoning normally requires the concurrent consideration of at least two premises in order to infer a consequence from them. One fairly obvious prediction that one might make is that people's ability to make appropriate inferences will reduce with the increasing complexity of the problems, since the information to be taken into account may exceed working memory capacity. For example, we might expect people who show competence with individual inferences to make mistakes when a problem requires a chain of such inferences to be put together.

One influential theory of working memory is that proposed originally by Baddeley and Hitch (1974), which has stimulated much research and has also been subject to much reformulation (see Baddeley, 1986). The details of the theory do not concern us here, but it is relevant to note that its authors claimed evidence that manipulations designed to add loads to working memory caused differential disruption to verbal reasoning problems according to their linguistic complexity (e.g., Hitch & Baddeley, 1976). The reasoning problems they used were, however, of a very simple nature and later study of similar manipulations on more complex conditional reasoning problems failed to provide clear evidence for the theory (Evans & Brooks, 1981; Brooks, 1984). Johnson-Laird (personal communication) and his colleagues have experienced similar failure to disrupt spatial reasoning by the use of interference tasks.

The notion of working memory in reasoning has also been discussed by Johnson-Laird (e.g., 1983; Johnson-Laird & Bara, 1984) in application to his mental models theory of syllogistic inference. He does not propose a specific theory of working memory, but assumes that it has a limited capacity and works on a "first in first out" principle. The application to mental models theory is as follows. The theory assumes that people draw deductive inferences by attempting to construct an exhaustive set of mental models of possible situations described in the premises of the argument. Any additional relationships which are true in *all* models can be inferred as valid conclusions. Johnson-Laird and Bara demonstrate that the premises of the classical syllogisms require either one, two, or three mental models to be constructed. On the basis of limited working memory capacity they formed the hypothesis that fallacies were more likely to occur on problems requiring more models to be considered—a prediction supported by their experimental data.

Whilst the evidence for the role of working memory in reasoning is limited, it is clearly an important concept which should be kept in mind as a possible cause of error and bias in reasoning, especially when quantity or complexity of problem information appears to be causing significant disruption. Having examined this and several other ideas concerning possible causes of bias in reasoning, it is time to consider some empirical case studies. The two phenomena to be discussed are relatively well researched and contrastive in nature: the former concerns deductive reasoning and a bias reflecting attention to a formally irrelevant feature of the problem, whereas the latter concerns statistical inference and a *lack* of attention to a *relevant* feature.

EMPIRICAL CASE STUDIES

Matching Bias in Propositional Reasoning

Like many interesting phenomena "matching bias" was discovered by complete accident. As a postgraduate research student, I decided to investigate reasoning using conditional statements which included negative as well as affirmative components. In one experiment (Evans, 1972b) I investigated subjects' ability to construct "truth tables" for such rules. The subjects were shown a display of coloured geometric figures drawn on cards and given rules of the form: "If there is (not) a red triangle on the left, then there is (not) a green square on the right." Each subject was presented with four rules in all in which the presence and absence of a negative in either the antecedent or consequent component of the rule was varied, as were the particular cards to which the rules referred. For each rule they were given both a verification task and a falsification task. The former involved picking out all pairs of cards (or generalising verbally to save time) which made the rule true, whilst the latter involved specifying all possible falsifying combinations. For example, if the rule was "If there is a red triangle on the left then there is not a green square on the right", a subject might place a red triangle next to a blue circle in order to confirm the rule, and then indicate that any figure on the right, other than a green square, would do just as well.

The purpose of the experiment was to test the earlier claim of Wason (1966) that people regard conditional statements as *irrelevant*—rather than as true or false—when the antecedent condition is false. For example, the rule "If it is a dog then it has four legs" may appear true for a four-legged dog, false for a three-legged dog, but irrelevant to tables and chairs regardless of their numbers of legs. Evidence for this hypothesis was provided by Johnson-Laird and Tagart (1969) by asking subjects directly to evaluate possible truth contingencies by rating them as true, false or irrelevant. My own experiment was designed to improve on their methodology by using a construction rather than evaluation task. The point was that any subject failing to construct a particular logical case either when verifying or falsifying could be *inferred* to consider that case irrelevant, without being cued explicitly to make a relevance judgement.

The four logical cases can be summarised as TT, TF, FT and FF according to whether or not the antecedent and consequent conditions of the conditional are true or false (see Fig. 2.2 for a concrete example). The experiment was designed to find out whether people evaluate conditionals according to the "defective truth table" proposed by Wason (1966)—that is rating TT as true, TF as false, but ignoring FT and FF as irrelevant (in standard two value logic the latter would be regarded as true). On this basis, I predicted (Evans, 1972b) that the cases with false antecedents would tend not to be

If there is a blue square on the left,
then there is not a green diamond on the right.

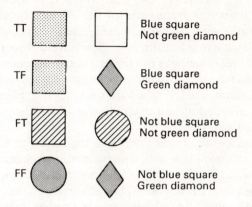

FIG. 2.2.   Example of truth table cases for a conditional rule of the type used by Evans (1972b).

constructed as either verifying or falsifying cases by the subjects. In general, this was confirmed, but the really interesting finding was that subjects' choices were massively influenced by the presence and absence of negative components in the rules, revealing a hitherto unknown cause of perceived relevance which I dubbed "matching bias".

Consider, for example, the TF case which, by any logical view, must falsify the rule since the antecedent is observed in the absence of the consequent. When the rule presented had a negative consequent, for example, "If there is a blue square on the left, then there is not a green diamond on the right", 23 of the 24 subjects placed a blue square next to a green diamond when asked to falsify the rule. This is the TF case and hence logically correct. However when the negative was in the antecedent of the rule, subjects' response to the falsification task was very different. For example, assuming the rule was, "If there is not a red square on the left then there is a yellow circle on the right" only 7 out of 24 initially chose a TF combination, e.g. by placing a green square (not a red square) next to a blue diamond (not a yellow circle). Instead, 15 subjects offered the FT combination, i.e. a red square next to a yellow circle. The bias involved is obvious: subjects prefer to choose the cards actually named in the rules and find it hard to see the relevance of instances which match neither the antecedent nor consequent values named. As evidence of the strength of the bias, only two subjects offered FT cases for initial falsification on the other three rules put together!

Now what could be the cause of this "matching bias"? Pollard (1982) has suggested that "subjects appear to respond with the 'available' stimuli embedded in the task instructions". There are, however, a number of difficulties

with a simple availability explanation. Firstly, the bias affected only the falsification task in the Evans (1972b) study: on the verification task subjects
showed a near universal preference for the TT case on all rules, including
those of the form *If not p then not q* which require choice of two cards which
fail to match those named in the rule. Secondly, subsequent research has
shown that the phenomenon is not limited to construction tasks, but is equally manifest on truth table evaluation tasks (see e.g., several experiments by
Brooks, 1984). Evans (1975) in fact showed that the subjective truth tables
produced by construction and evaluation methodologies followed a near
identical distribution.

The significance of the latter findings is this: subjects who fail to select a
case on the construction task will, with near equal frequency, explicitly describe the equivalent case as "irrelevant" on an evaluation task. Hence, the
construction task data cannot be explained simply on the basis that subjects
pick out the "available" (matching) cases but rather indicate that matching
is a determinant of their perceived *relevance*. But why should matching cases
appear relevant, and why should the bias affect falsification rather than verification judgements?

Recently (Evans, 1983b; 1984a) I put forward a linguistic hypothesis to
explain the effect with reference to the topic/comment distinction. The argument is that the propositions included in a statement form the topic while
modifiers such as negatives affect only the comment. For example, the statements "I am writing a book" and "I am not writing a book" have the same
topic but a different comment. Hence, in a linguistic sense a sentence of the
form "If (not) p then (not) q" is always about p and q regardless of the presence of negatives. Logically, of course, the statement is about the connection between two propositions including any negations. The reason for the
lack of effect of matching on the verification task is that it is overridden by
another, more powerful linguistic factor—that stemming from the understanding of the word *if*. The use of *if* invites one to entertain the supposition
that the antecedent condition is true (cf. Rips & Marcus, 1977). In other
words the listener is strongly invited to consider the hypothesis (mental
model, possible world) in which the antecedent and consequent conditions
are actually fulfilled (i.e. the TT case).

In summary, I propose that people's evaluations of conditional statements
are strongly influenced by two linguistic determinants of perceived relevance. An item named is likely to appear relevant whether asserted or denied
(matching bias) but a proposition, including a negation, is likely to appear
relevant if it is the subject of a conditional sentence. I have been able to
provide some direct supporting evidence for this theory in recently published experiments. For example, in one study (Evans, 1983b) the instances
were described by statements using explicit negatives (e.g., "The letter is A
and the number is not 4") such that the conditional statements and the in-

stances always referred to the same items. This lead, as predicted, to a large and significant decrease in the amount of matching bias observed relative to a control group. Another study involved the Wason selection task, a different conditional reasoning problem also known to be vulnerable to matching bias (see Chapter Four for a description). Evans, Ball, and Brooks (1987) observed the order in which people made decisions and found that matching items were considered before mismatching ones, hence supporting the hypothesis that these receive preferential attention.

There are other reasons for believing that matching bias reflects a complex, linguistically determined relevance judgement rather than a simply availability or response priming effect. If it were the latter, for example, one would expect the effect to generalise across linguistic contexts. In fact, matching bias does occur when subjects evaluate statements of the form "p only if q" (e.g. Evans, 1975; Evans & Newstead, 1977) but does *not* occur when a disjunctive statement of the form "p or q" is used (see Evans & Newstead, 1980). In retrospect, I believe that the absence of matching bias in disjunctive reasoning is due to the different linguistic context which they induce relative to conditionals. A conditional ("if...then" or "...only if...") is essentially hypothetical in nature, so that it seems to the subject that the rule might or might not apply. That is why subjects use three truth values—true, false, and irrelevant for evaluation of such sentences. It was noticeable in the Evans and Newstead (1980) experiment that the proportion of irrelevant or non-constructed cases was much lower than with conditionals.

Clearly the matching bias effect provides a good example of errors in reasoning arising from selective processing of the problem information and provides a good fit to the heuristic/analytic distinction proposed by Evans (1984a). A logically irrelevant feature of the problem is inducing selective attention to, and perceived relevance of certain information. However, it is important to note also that matching status does *not* influence the choice between true and false classifications of cases considered relevant on the truth table task. Those decisions take clear account of the logical relationship of the case to the rule, in line with the second stage "analytic" processes proposed by Evans (1984a). This brief review has also illustrated the complexities involved in understanding the causes of such an apparently simple and replicable bias such as matching. It does, however, provide interesting evidence that verbal reasoning may be subject to powerful non-logical influences arising from linguistic comprehension processes.

Understanding the Law of Large Numbers

The law of large numbers is a statistical law which is quite simple to state and understand. A random sample will estimate the characteristics of the population from which it is drawn with increasing accuracy as the size of the sample increases. Since the benefits of additional sampling provide a diminishing return (measurement error actually reducing with the square root of the sample size) we can say that satisfactory estimates can be obtained when the sample size is sufficiently large—hence the law of large numbers. The problem most frequently arises when we wish to estimate either a proportion or a mean. For example, an opinion poll survey may be aimed at investigating the proportions of the population inclined to vote for different political parties. A survey based on 1000 voters will produce much more reliable estimates than one based on 100. On the other hand, a sample of 2000 voters may provide only small additional accuracy, not justifying its additional cost.

The question of what precise number constitutes a sufficiently large sample for a given problem depends on a number of factors specific to the situation under consideration. Interestingly, studies of intuitive statistical judgement concerned with sample size have concentrated exclusively on the question of whether people overestimate the power of small samples and I know of no studies addressing themselves directly to the issue of whether people understand the diminishing return from ever larger samples. In fact, both aspects of the intuition are of practical importance since optimal decision behaviour requires one to sample sufficiently but not excessively. For example, most psychologists choose the sample sizes for their experiments on the basis of intuition or tradition rather than with the aid of formal calculation. The sample size chosen is a crucial determinant of the statistical power or sensitivity of the design—i.e. the chance of obtaining a statistically significant result given that the effect being tested for is, in fact, present. If the sample size chosen is too low, then effects may easily be missed as the measurements are swamped with the large random variations to be expected with small samples. On the other hand if the sample size chosen is excessive with respect to effects of the size that interest the investigator then time and money will clearly be wasted.

The importance of an intuitive appreciation of the effects of sample size is quite general to human judgement and inference and by no means restricted to those who conduct formal statistical surveys and experiments. In essence, life involves a series of inductive inferences as we attempt constantly to form and maintain our beliefs about the world by generalising from our experiences. Hence any general insensitivity to the size—or bias—of samples of evidence in social cognition could clearly lead to the formation of inaccurate world beliefs including various forms of prejudice. Consequently, a number of psychological studies have addressed themselves to the apparently straightforward question of whether or not people possess an intuitive rule corresponding to the law of large numbers. As is often the case in psychological research, the answer turns out to be a good deal more complicated than the question!

The strongest claims that people lack intuitive understanding of the law of large numbers have been made by Amos Tversky and Daniel Kahneman, although they later moderated their views (cf. Kahneman & Tversky, 1982a). Tversky and Kahneman (1971) reported various experiments including ones which showed that psychologists significantly overestimate the power of research designs based on small sample sizes and put forward the general claim that people hold a belief in the "law of small numbers". The following year saw the publication by Kahneman and Tversky (1972b) of the proposal of the "representativeness" heuristic and a series of experiments supporting their claim that subjects apparently have no appreciation at all of the effects of sample size on statistical inferences.

Representativeness is the major alternative heuristic to availability that has been proposed by Kahneman and Tversky to form the basis of intuitive statistical judgement. It is concerned with judgements about the likelihood of samples being drawn from populations, or events occurring given some particular hypothesis. People are said to judge the likelihood of an uncertain event or sample by "the degree to which it is similar in essential properties to the parent population". Since sample size is a feature of the sample only, it cannot influence a judgement of similarity with the population. Hence, it is the similarity of essential features such as means and proportions which determine representativeness, with sample size ignored entirely.

Kahneman and Tversky (1972b) presented a series of experiments on intuitive statistical judgement in which subjects did indeed ignore sample size altogether. However, subsequent research has modified this picture considerably. Whilst their experiments are replicable in their original form, a number of studies have shown that subjects may well take account of sample size if the form of the problems is modified or when the variable is manipulated in alternative tasks. A good example, involves the maternity hospital problem which was presented by Kahneman and Tversky (1972b, p.443) in the following form:

A certain town is served by two hospitals. In the larger hospital about 45 babies are born each day, and in the smaller hospital about 15 babies are born each day. As you know about 50% of all babies are boys. The exact percentage of baby boys, however, varies from day to day. Sometimes it may be higher than 50%, sometimes lower.
For a period of one year, each hospital recorded the days on which (more/less) than 60% of the babies born were boys. Which hospital do you think recorded more such days?

Subjects were allowed to express a preference for either hospital or else to indicate indifference. Those expressing a preference were divided randomly between the two hospitals regardless of which way the question was posed. This appears to show a clear lack of understanding of the law of large numbers which clearly implies that the smaller hospital will more often experience the deviant result specified—i.e. that more than 60% of the babies born are boys.

Evans and Dusoir (1977) replicated Kahneman and Tversky's finding with the maternity hospital problem in its original form, but found that a significant majority of subjects could solve the problem when the wording was simplified. In the simplest form, subjects were asked to decide which hospital was more likely to observe on one day that all the babies born were boys. In a forced choice 85% of subjects correctly indicated that this was more likely with the smaller hospital. Bar-Hillel (1979) also facilitated performance on this problem by simplifying the wording. Strong evidence was also presented by Olson (1976) that neglect of sample size on some of the other tasks described by Kahneman and Tversky (1972b) was due to factors—including complexity of instructions—other than representativeness.

If the null results reported by Kahneman and Tversky (1972b) were due to subjects' difficulties in understanding the instructions does that mean that subjects do understand the law of large numbers after all? Well, yes—and no! As with base rates, subjects are most likely to take account of sample size if it is the only variable specified in the problem. For example, Evans and Dusoir (1975) found near 100% correct responding when asking subjects whether a statistical estimate based on a small or large sample was more likely to produce an accurate result. Judgements may, however, be influenced by the presence of other factors which appear to the subject to be relevant to the judgement, although generally speaking some normative appreciation of the effects of sample size can still be demonstrated.

For example, subjects can be asked to assess relative probabilities of binomial samples occurring under the null hypothesis. Evans and Dusoir (1977; Evans and Pollard, 1982) asked subjects to judge which of various pairings of experimental results of tossing a coin gave better evidence of a biased coin, e.g. they might be asked to compare an outcome of 8 heads to 2 tails with one of 70 heads to 30 tails. All else being equal subjects tend correctly to judge that samples with larger size or with larger proportional differences give better evidence of bias. However, when the two factors are put into conflict people generally overweight the proportionality factor such that many would erroneously think in the above example that 8 out of 10 is a less likely outcome for a fair coin than 70 out of 100, while the truth lies dramatically in the opposite direction. This overweighting of proportionality might be regarded as weak evidence for the representativeness hypothesis.

Evans and Pollard (1985) reported a study in which subjects were asked to make intuitive assessments of the likelihood of normally distributed data samples which varied in: (1) difference between the sample mean and that of the population; (2) variability around the sample mean; and (3) size of the sample. As with binomial judgements, probability estimates generally moved in the right direction with all three factors. Hence, subjects appreciated that mean differences in the sample were more significant when the sample size was greater and less significant when the sample variability was larger. That is not to say that they were accurate, since the absolute level of their probability estimates were extremely conservative—i.e. subjects considerably *underestimated* the power of the relatively large samples presented. There were also presentation effects in this study of direct relevance to the availability/relevance notions discussed earlier in this chapter. More weighting was given to sample size when numerical rather than histogram displays of samples were used, whereas sample variance was taken into account more with the latter type of display. This appears to be a salience effect in so far as the (percentage) histograms emphasised the variability by the visual spread on the screen whereas sample size was much more visible in the condition where a block of numbers was shown.

One logically *irrelevant* factor has also been shown to influence people's intuitions about sample size, namely that of population size. Bar-Hillel (1979) proposed that subjects might believe the representativeness of samples to be based on the sample to population ratio rather than on the absolute sample size as is actually the case. She found evidence for this in a task where subjects had to express confidence in samples drawn from towns whose population size was stated. Subjects were more confident in samples of smaller absolute size if they accounted for a larger proportion of the population. This fallacy was confirmed by Evans and Bradshaw (1986) using an alternative methodology. In the latter study subjects played the role of quality control researchers choosing an appropriate sample size for a study. Subjects specified considerably larger samples when the population to be studied was larger with mean estimates of sample required approaching the 2:1 ratio in population size. It is interesting to note that the absolute size of samples specified were also considerably *larger* than those computed to be actually necessary according to the conditions of the problem. In conjunction with the conservative absolute judgements reported by Evans and Pollard (1985) this suggests that subjects may indeed underestimate the value of large samples as well as sometimes overestimating the probity of small ones.

It is quite clear from the evidence discussed that people do exhibit some intuitive understanding of the law of large numbers in psychological experiments, but that the reliability and extent of this intuition is dependent upon how instructions are phrased and what other factors are manipulated in the problems. More generally, Nisbett, Krantz, Jepson, and Kunda (1983) have argued, with experimental evidence, that everyday inductive reasoning may employ either statistical or non-statistical heuristics according to the perceived clarity of the statistical structure of the problem and cultural conventions related to the domain. Not surprisingly, Kahneman and Tversky

(1982a) have also rethought their position on the law of large numbers in the light of accumulated experimental evidence, and now suggest that subjects may understand the rule but frequently fail to apply it. Significantly, they also suggest that such rules may not be held in a general abstract manner but embodied in context-dependent schemas. Detailed discussion of this kind of approach will be given in Chapter Five.

What does the study of intuitions about sample size tell us about the main theoretical concern of this chapter, namely the role of selective processing in reasoning? In particular, why is evidence concerning sample size taken into account in some situations but ignored in others? First of all, we have seen that complexity of instructional presentation can critically affect ability to utilise an embedded logically relevant piece of information. In the case of the maternity hospital problem it is quite striking that a small change of wording can have such a big influence on correct responding. A possible explanation here is that subjects attempt to formulate a mental model but that the complexity of trying to construct and maintain in working memory cases of "more than 60% boys" defeats them leading to a random response. On the other hand they can run a mental simulation to look for cases of "all boys" and see that this will occur more often with the smaller hospitals. An alternative explanation is that subjects simply fail to encode the event specified as an "unrepresentative outcome" unless it is simply described. The latter explanation assumes that people have a rule but can only apply it if the relevant data are correctly encoded. The mental models approach, on the other hand, denies the existence of a rule *per se* but suggests instead that the law of large numbers emerges as a property of the mental simulation.

The presentation factors investigated by Evans and Pollard (1985) provide clear evidence of how selective processing of problem information may be induced. A finding not mentioned above was that subjects—when tested directly—were equally able to *perceive* the variability of samples presented in either format, but were more likely to take this factor into account in their probability judgements when the display enhanced its salience. This suggests that some kind of vividness or relevance effect is operating, not simply an availability bias. It is also interesting how the tendency to take account of sample size is influenced also by the presence of other factors. Why is it, for example, that if subjects think population size is such a relevant variable when it is available, that they will nevertheless happily make judgements about sample size on tasks where this information is not stated and never think to request it?

It is hard to avoid the conclusion that human subjects are rather passive in their reasoning processes, responding to whatever is presented without really thinking about anything which is not brought to their attention. While people's inferences may sometimes be affected by the logically relevant factors, they may also fallaciously latch on to irrelevant information—such as population size—if it is made available to them. Some intuitions, whilst logically correct, are fragile and liable to easy distraction. Hence, understanding of the importance of base rates is usually demolished by the presence of specific evidence and that of sample size is diminished by the presence of information about sample proportions.

CONCLUSIONS

It is apparent from both the case studies and other psychological experiments discussed in this chapter that people exhibit enormously variable levels of observed competence when tested for understanding of a logical or statistical principle. At one time reasoning researchers appeared to believe that people either did or did not "possess" a given rule and that all that was required was to present people with a problem requiring use of the rule and see whether or not they solved it. The dangers of this approach are all too evident from the example of experimentation on the law of large numbers which has produced all extremes of observed competence, from problems where everyone appears to understand the rule to those on which no-one appears to understand it! However, simply to take recourse in the competence/performance distinction and say that man is rational after all (in the manner of Cohen, 1981) misses the point. The task for the psychologist is to form a theory of knowledge and reasoning capable of specifying the conditions under which such competence will or will not be manifest. I would, however, accept that the competence/performance distinction is important in that a complete psychological theory must address both aspects.

The argument between proponents of inference rules, schemas and mental models (cf. Chapter One) is essentially about the competence mechanism for reasoning. Important and interesting though the competence issue is, it is a central assumption of this book that it is possible to make progress in understanding the nature of reasoning performance—in particular the attendant errors and biases—in the absence of a clear resolution of the competence issue. The main emphasis in the present chapter has been on the mechanisms which may cause selective encoding and usage of relevant and irrelevant information with clear consequences for the accuracy of the process of reasoning—however performed. In addition, the case studies have suggested some of the characteristics of problems such as complexity, linguistic factors, perceptual salience, and presence of competing features which appear to trigger such selective processing mechanisms.

3 Confirmation Bias

Confirmation bias is perhaps the best known and most widely accepted notion of inferential error to have come out of the literature on human reasoning. The claim, endorsed by a number of authors, is that human beings have a fundamental tendency to seek information consistent with their current beliefs, theories or hypotheses and to avoid the collection of potentially falsifying evidence. Numerous laboratory experiments have seemingly shown that subjects fail to discover general rules when required actively to seek relevant evidence because they adopt strategies designed to confirm rather than refute their hypotheses.

Interest in the phenomenon of confirmation bias is widespread. It is, for example, identified by Baron (1985) as one of the central problems to be overcome in the attempt to facilitate the use of rational strategies in human thought. In social cognition, confirmation bias may be seen as a major mechanism responsible for the maintenance of prejudice and irrational beliefs. Most particularly, however, Peter Wason and a number of other authors whose work will be discussed in this chapter have argued that the bias operates directly against the dictates of Popper and other philosophers of science concerning the correct means of conducting scientific enquiry. Scientists should attempt to falsify their theories and to examine alternative hypotheses wherever possible, whereas intelligent student subjects in laboratory simulations of scientific reasoning generally appear to do the precise reverse.

In this chapter, I will examine much of the central evidence for confirmation bias, especially that based upon simulations of scientific reasoning. Whilst there is no doubt that the reasoning task performances in question are subject to error and biases, I should make it clear from the outset that my interpretation of these experiments differs from the shared assumptions of most researchers in the field. The view which appears to prevail in the literature is that confirmatory behaviour reflects a kind of motivational bias. For whatever reason—vanity, maintenance of belief structures, etc. —subjects are assumed to be actively attempting to verify rather than falsify their hypotheses. My view, on the contrary, is that the phenomena associated with studies of confirmation bias reflect not a motivational bias but a set of cognitive failures. Subjects confirm, not because they want to, but because they cannot think of the way to falsify. The cognitive failure is caused by a form of selective processing which is very fundamental indeed in cognition—a bias to think about positive rather than negative information. For want of a better term I will refer to this as a "positivity bias". In support of the existence of such a positivity bias are many studies showing profound difficulties experienced by subjects in comprehending and processing linguistic and logical negations (see, for example, Evans, 1982, Chapter Two). Not only do I believe a general positivity bias to underlie the phenomena normally referred to as "confirmation bias" but I believe this fundamental cause of selective processing to be closely connected to other phenomena such as the matching bias effect introduced in Chapter Two.

Positivity bias, in line with other explanations of bias proposed in this book, is assumed to arise from preconscious heuristic processes which determine the locus of subjects' attention. It is not a deliberate or conscious strategy of the kind described recently by Klayman and Ha (1987) as a "positive test heuristic". The nature of positivity bias will be explicated further in the course of this chapter in which the experiments and arguments of various authors will be closely examined, and the relation to the theory of Klayman and Ha will be discussed at the end of the chapter. First, however, a brief discussion of the nature of scientific thinking is required, since it is this problem which motivates the design of most of the relevant research studies.

THE NATURE OF SCIENTIFIC INFERENCE

I will look only at those aspects of scientific thought which involve logical reasoning, namely the testing and elimination of theories and hypotheses. The creative thought processes of scientists which lead to the formation of new theories and discovery of new ideas are beyond the scope of the present book. Readers interested in a fuller treatment of the subject of scientific thinking are referred to the work of Tweney, Doherty, and Mynatt (1981).

Scientific activity is divided roughly into two main areas: theory and experiment. All sciences involve collection of empirical evidence or data according to agreed methodologies, frequently under controlled laboratory conditions. The simple accumulation of data does not, however, constitute science. The state of knowledge in a given field is formulated as one or more theories. It is the theories which generally motivate the design of scientific research and which are used to interpret or make sense of the data which are collected. The exact purpose of scientific activity is not, however, self-evident and has been a subject of debate in the history and philosophy of science.

The obvious purpose of science would appear to be the discovery of the "truth" about the natural world. A good scientific theory can be used to make predictions and calculations about the real world which are sufficiently accurate for the many practical applications which we see in the form of various technologies. A strong tradition in the philosophy of science, especially within the Empiricist and Positivist schools, holds that empirical observations are the only true source of knowledge about the world and that scientific laws and principles are in essence empirical generalisations. However, this view creates the problem that the basic mechanism of scientific inference would appear to be that of inductive generalisation. That is to say the laws are discovered or inferred from many observations of phenomena which conform to them. Hence, for example, one might suppose that there is a "law of gravity" whose nature can be safely inferred from the repeated observation of the behaviour of objects falling towards the centre of the earth.

The logical difficulty with this approach, known as the problem of induction, is that to which the philosopher Karl Popper (1959; 1962) proposed a famous and highly influential solution. To explain the problem we must return to the distinction between inductive and deductive reasoning. Whilst inferences can be made deductively from general principles to particular cases, the reverse process of necessity involves induction. Consider a general, or universal statement such as: "All metals expand when heated". If this claim is held to be true, then you could reason that since copper, for example, is a metal it will expand when heated. This is a valid, deductive inference. It can be demonstrated in logic that this conclusion must be true provided that the assumptions upon which it is based are sound.

An inductive generalisation, on the other hand, runs along the lines "all the metals that I have heated were observed to expand, therefore all metals expand when heated". This sort of reasoning, as with any type of inductive inference, is clearly not logically valid. There may be some metal, as yet undiscovered which does not expand, or there may be some condition which you failed to include in your experiments under which one or more metals would fail to comply with the law. The problem of induction is that science would appear to be based upon unsound reasoning, since a general claim can never be proved, with certainty, to be true.

Popper's solution to this problem was to reject inductive generalisation as the methodology of science. Although a general rule cannot be proved by an unlimited number of confirmatory observations it can be disproved by a single disconfirmatory observation. It I heat copper and it fails to expand then the claim is evidently false. Whilst verification of universal claims depends upon unsound inductive inference, falsification is based on a deductive inference of the following form: "Assuming that all metals expand when heated, it follows that copper, being a metal, will do so. If copper fails to expand when heated then it follows that the theory is incorrect". The general form of this argument is known in formal logic as *Modus Tollens*. Given any assertion of the form *If p then q,* and an observation that q is false, it follows that p must be false. In the case of science, p represents a theory and q a prediction deduced from it. Failure to observe q, entails the falsity of p. (Observing q, on the other hand does not prove p to be true—a fallacy of reasoning known as Affirmation of the Consequent.) In practice theories usually consist of a number of assumptions, in which case a failed prediction implies that at least one of the assumptions was incorrect. Hence, theories are frequently modified, rather than abandoned, in the face of falsifying evidence.

Popper's approach to science is then essentially deductive. He argues that a theory is not scientific at all unless it is potentially falsifiable, and advocates an approach to science which requires active attempts to falsify theories. Hence, scientific theories evolve through a process akin to natural selection. Those which fail to predict the evidence are eliminated or revised. There are no "true" theories, only theories which have survived thus far because they perform better than rival accounts on the evidence available to date. Whilst there are, of course, alternative philosophies of science to Popper's, his notion of falsification as a fundamental strategy in scientific research has achieved widespread acceptance among psychologists and other scientists. For this reason, there has been considerable interst in a number of psychological experiments which involve subjects in testing hypotheses—the literature which has led to the belief that people exhibit an anti-Popperian confirmation bias.

The studies considered in this chapter are principally those in the cognitive tradition which examine active seeking of information by subjects. They are mostly concerned with the question of whether subjects attempt to prove or disprove a claim, but also provide some findings on what people do when confronted with falsifying evidence. These experiments actually provide a relatively weak test of confirmation bias in real life, since they have not generally asked subjects to test hypotheses about which they hold real world beliefs. Whilst there are a large number of areas of research in social psychology concerning belief maintenance which could be deemed relevant to the general concept of confirmation bias, it is beyond the scope of this book to review this literature. However, a related phenomenon, known as belief bias, which refers to the tendency of prior beliefs and attitudes to distort people's reasoning, will be considered in detail in Chapter Four.

WASON'S 2 4 6 PROBLEM

Wason (1960) presented an apparently simple reasoning task which produced very interesting results. Subjects were told that the experimenter had a rule in mind which classifies sets of three integers (whole numbers). I will refer to such groups of three numbers as "triples" in this discussion. In the original form of the task, subjects were told that the triple "2 4 6" conformed to the rule. They were then asked to try to discover the rule by generating triples of their own. For each triple, the experimenter told the subject whether or not it conformed to his rule. Subjects kept a written record of their triples, the experimenter's responses, and their current hypotheses about the rule. They were told not to announce the rule until they were sure of its correctness. If they announced a wrong rule then they were told so and asked to continue testing triples.

The example 2 4 6 was deliberately chosen to suggest a specific sort of rule to the subject such as "Ascending with equal intervals", whereas the actual rule held by the experimenter was "Any ascending sequence". Subjects found the task surprisingly difficult. The majority announced at least one incorrect hypothesis and a substantial minority failed to solve it at all. What has created the interest in this task, however, is the pattern of hypothesis testing behaviour which emerged. In general, subjects test their hypotheses by testing only positive examples, with the consequence that they fail to receive disconfirming evidence. If, for example, the subject has the hypothesis that the rule is "Ascending with equal intervals" and tests triples such as 10 12 14, 10 20 30, 1 2 3, and 100 500 900, the experimenter will, of course, in each case respond that the triple conforms to his rule. Subjects thus receive consistent evidence for their hypothesis, become convinced of its correctness and are very puzzled when told it is wrong. What they generally don't do is to test examples such as 100 200 500 which do not conform with the hypothesis. Such negative predictions would lead to falsification of the hypothesis since the experimenter would still say that they conformed with his rule. The phenomenon is very reliable and can be demonstrated informally by trying this experiment with some friends.

Wason claimed that subjects were exhibiting a verification or confirmation bias. In other words, contrary to Popperian dogma, they were attempting to find evidence which could confirm rather than falsify their current hypothesis. Whilst this claim has achieved, and continues to achieve widespread acceptance, it has also been criticised (Wetherick, 1962; Evans, 1983a; Klayman & Ha, 1987). To see why, we must examine the nature of

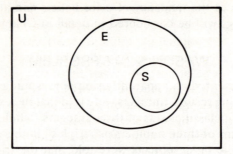

U   Universal set – all triples

E   Experimenter's rule – all
        triples in ascending sequence

S   Subject's rule – e.g. ascending
        with equal intervals

FIG. 3.1.   Set relationships on Wason's 2 4 6 problem.

the task a little more closely. There is no argument about the fact that subjects' problems on this task arise from their repeated acquisition of confirming evidence for incorrect hypotheses: the argument is about whether they
intend to achieve confirmation or whether their strategy is only ineffective
because of the particular nature of the task which induces a cognitive failure.

The subjects' problems stem from the fact that they are induced to form an
hypothesis which is a restricted or more specific version of the experimenter's rule (see Fig. 3.1). This means that any triple which conforms to their
hypothesis will also conform to the experimenter's rule. In a sense they hold
partially correct rules. The hypothesis "All triples ascending with equal intervals conform" is correct, but insufficiently generalised. To use a logical
distinction they show that their rule is a sufficient explanation of conforming
triples but not that it is a necessary one. They fail to test whether triples
which do not conform with their hypothesis could also be positive examples.

This failure to test negative examples of one's hypotheses is undoubtedly a
cognitive failure and an important one. Whether it demonstrates a confirmation bias, in a motivational sense is, however, moot. There are many situations where hypotheses could be eliminated by positive predictions which
fail. The subjects on the 2 4 6 problem are not to know that the logical
relation of their hypotheses to the experimenter's rule is such that falsification can only be achieved by a negative test. Some recent work using instructional sets to verify or falsify is relevant to this issue and will be discussed later in the chapter.

Before looking at more recent work, it is worth commenting on a very
interesting characteristic emphasised is early discussions of the 2 4 6 pro-

blem (e.g., Wason, 1967; Wason & Johnson-Laird, 1972) which has been somewhat neglected in later papers. The phenomenon is illustrated by a typical protocol from the original experiment (see Table 3.1). A number of subjects exhibited a tendency to present the same hypothesis repeatedly in alternative verbal formulations. Note that the second to fourth rules announced by this particular subject are all logically equivalent! At the very least this conveys the degree of fixation and subjective certainty which repeated verification of an hypothesis can create. Wason and Evans (1975) have taken this phenomenon, among others, as evidence for "dual thought processes", in which non-verbal, unconscious biases can cause verbal "rationalisations" to occur (see Chapter Five).

There is always a danger in psychology that results will turn out to be "paradigm-specific". In other words what may appear to be interesting psychological trends may be dependent upon some particular feature of a task. In the case of the 2 4 6 problem we have evidence that basic findings do generalise to other tasks of a similar logical structure. For example, an experiment by Penrose (described by Wason, 1967) used a verbal task where the experimenter's rule was "all living things" and the example given to the subjects of an object conforming to the rule was "a Siamese cat". The majority of subjects announced incorrect rules and showed the same pattern

TABLE 3.1
Sample Protocol from Wason (1960)

No.4. Female, aged 19, 1st year undergraduate

8 10 12: two added each time; 14 16 18: even numbers in order of magnitude; 20 22 24: same reason; 1 3 5: two added to preceding number.

The rule is that by starting with any number two is added each time to form the next number.

2 6 10: middle number is the arithmetic mean of the other two; 1 50 99: same reason.

The rule is that the middle number is the arithmetic mean of the other two.

3 10 17: same number, seven, added each time; 0 3 6: three added each time.

The rule is that the difference between two numbers next to each other is the same.

12 8 4: the same number subtracted each time to form the next number.

The rule is adding a number, always the same one to form the next number.

1 4 9: any three numbers in order of magnitude.

The rule is any three numbers in order of magnitude.

(17 minutes)

of fixation on particular hypotheses for which they repeatedly gathered confirming evidence. Like the 2 4 6, this task permits subjects to form hypotheses which are subsets of the actual rule, e.g. mammals.

A parallel finding was reported by Miller (1967) in a study with ostensibly quite different objectives. Miller was interested in how people learn the syntax of languages and created a task in which subjects had to discover the rules of an artificial grammar. Subjects had to type in strings of letters to an on-line computer which responded by classifying them as correct or incorrect. When they were sure that they had learned the rules of the grammar they were asked to take a test. Most failed for precisely the same sort of reason that subjects announce incorrect rules on the 2 4 6 problem. They discovered only a part of the grammar and repeatedly tested positive examples of their hypotheses receiving constant reinforcement. They failed on the test because they had only discovered a sufficient rule for generating legal examples and had not demonstrated its necessity. Other variants of the standard 2 4 6 task used in more recent papers will be described later in the chapter.

It may well be that the "confirmation bias" demonstrated on the 2 4 6 and related problems depends upon the fact that subjects are induced to form hypotheses which define a set of exemplars which are a subset of those defined by the true rule. In other words it may be that subjects are not attempting to confirm hypotheses *per se,* but are simply unable to think of testing them in a negative manner—in line with the postulated positivity bias. Nevertheless, it seems clear, for example from the protocol evidence, that subjects do become convinced of the veracity of false hypotheses and there are situations in science which could be modelled by tasks of this nature. In essence, the mistake is a failure to generalise. When a new phenomenon is observed it is likely to be a special case of something more general. If scientists, like subjects in these experiments, are satisfied with partial explanations of phenomena and are convinced by continuing confirming evidence then this might lead to serious error or at least unduly slow progress. The problem would not, however, be caused by a "confirmation bias" as such.

Psychologists in this field have been sufficiently concerned that a very general and serious bias of thought is involved that they have made a number of attempts to find means of removing the bias and inducing insight in their subjects, primarily by the use of different forms of instructions. These experiments relate to the question of whether people can be educated to be good Popperians and induced to test their hypotheses more effectively, and also provide evidence concerning the underlying cause of the phenomenon. Studies of this sort will now be considered in detail.

ATTEMPTING TO REMOVE CONFIRMATION BIAS

The studies discussed in this section are illustrative of attempts at "debiasing", a problem which will be examined more generally in Chapter Six. Recent interest in the phenomenon originally identified by Wason (1960) dates from the paper of Mynatt, Doherty, and Tweney (1977) who introduced a task which they felt would improve on the 2 4 6 problem as a simulation of scientific hypothesis testing. They created an artificial "universe", via a series of graphical displays on an on-line computer. Subjects were shown displays of simple geometric shapes and were able to "fire particles" at any location to observe their effect. The rule to be discovered was that particles would be "absorbed" when hitting invisible boundaries which surrounded figures of a given brightness level. Subjects were, however, given initial screens in which brightness level was confounded with shape, in the hope of inducing an incorrect hypothesis that triangular shapes were responsible (the authors assumed that shape would be more salient than brightness). Subjects were required to write down their hypotheses before proceeding further.

In the next phase of the experiment subjects were asked to choose between pairs of screens for testing. Six of these pairs were designed so that one could produce only confirmatory evidence for a subject holding the triangle hypothesis (in the confirmatory screens the only figures of the correct brightness were triangles). Subjects were divided into three groups according to the instructional set given. One group was instructed to try to confirm their hypothesis, one to disconfirm, and the other simply to test their hypotheses.

The study produced several clear findings. First, subjects who formed the initial triangle hypothesis did show a clear bias towards seeking confirmatory evidence. Second, this confirmation bias was not affected by the instructions given. Finally, it was found that when subjects did encounter falsifying evidence they generally did reject their hypotheses. These findings suggest that subjects may be passive rather than active Popperians. That is to say they recognise the significance of falsifying evidence and respond accordingly, but they fail actively to seek out such evidence. Apparent parallels in research on Wason's selection task will be noted later in the chapter.

A second study by the same authors produced somewhat different results, however. Mynatt, Doherty, and Tweney (1978) modified their procedure in two main ways: (1) hypothetical universes were again simulated by an interactive graphical program but the logical task was made more complex, and (2) the instructional manipulation was made more powerful. One group was given extensive written instructions emphasising the importance of falsification and the need to test multiple hypotheses and was given a copy of Platt's

(1964) discussion of "strong inference" to read. There was a control group who received no such instructions. There was also a procedural modification in that subjects were instructed to "think aloud" so that verbal protocols could be tape recorded.

The construction of the task in this study made it difficult to tell whether or not subjects were seeking to confirm their hypotheses. However, in clear contrast with the results of Mynatt et al. (1977), subjects showed a clear tendency to resist falsifying evidence, frequently maintaining hypotheses which were inconsistent with the evidence. It seems clear that this is due to the extra complexity of the task which no subject in fact solved. Perhaps the task was too complex in this study. The protocols cited in the paper suggest that subjects were fairly confused and holding on to their hypotheses for lack of inspiration concerning alternatives.

At this point it is worth noting some general findings of the substantial literature which has investigated inductive reasoning via the paradigm known as "concept identification" (cf. Bourne, Dominowski, & Loftus, 1979; Cohen & Murphy, 1984). On such tasks subjects are usually asked to discover rules by examining both positive and negative exemplars. The problems use rules which are generally clearly and quite simply defined and—contrary to the types of task reviewed here—will usually result in positive tests of incorrect hypotheses leading quite quickly to the discovery of disconfirming evidence. In the concept identification literature subjects almost invariably reject hypotheses once such falsifying evidence is encountered (e.g., Levine, 1966).

Mynatt et al. (1978) once again found that instructional set had no effect, suggesting that confirmation bias may be resistant to education. A partial success for instructional manipulation was, however, recorded by Tweney, Doherty, Warner, and Pliske (1980) who reverted to study of Wason's original 2 4 6 problem. By use of tape recorded protocols, Tweney et al. classified subjects' tests as intending to confirm or disconfirm their hypotheses. By this measure instructions were successful, i.e. subjects instructed to disconfirm attempted to do so. However, they did not solve the task significantly more often as a result—a rather curious finding for which the authors do not provide any clear explanation.

A series of recent studies by Michael Gorman and colleagues have also manipulated instructional set with rather mixed results. Gorman and Gorman (1984) managed to induce more successful problem solving as well as more disconfirmatory tests by use of instructions on the 2 4 6 problem. They suggested that the reason Tweney et al. failed to find this was that the latter authors, unlike Gorman and Gorman themselves, had provided feedback to subjects who announced incorrect hypotheses about the rule. Gorman and Gorman also used a tighter technique for measuring subjects' intentions by asking them to predict before each test whether the triple would be correct or incorrect (by the experimenters' rule). Subjects instructed to disconfirm, both predicted and obtained more incorrect triples than control subjects or those given confirmatory instructions.

Gorman, Gorman, Latta, and Cunningham (1984) introduced a new task called "New Eleusis" in which subjects had to try to discover a rule about playing cards by choosing them in sequence. The experimenter placed the cards horizontally or vertically on a table according to their correctness so that a complete record was visible at all times. This study also differed from others in that the problems were solved by small groups of subjects in collaboration. In the second experiment (but not the first) groups given disconfirmatory instructions—i.e. told to attempt to choose *incorrect* cards—solved significantly more problems. However, more recent studies have not succeeded in demonstrating a beneficial effect of instructions: these include a study by Gorman (1986) using a variant of New Eleusis in which subjects were told (falsely) that feedback on correctness was less than 100% reliable, and another by Gorman, Stafford, and Gorman (1987, Experiment I) using a "more difficult" 2 4 6 task in which an even more general rule than the usual one—no two numbers the same—had to be discovered.

The instructional manipulation is clearly relevant to the question of whether or not confirmation bias is motivational. If, as is generally assumed in the literature, the bias reflects an intention to confirm rather than falsify then one might well expect some benefit from the repeated and intensive efforts of experimenters to instruct a disconfirming strategy in their subjects. As we have seen, however, few studies have succeeded in improving performance though rather more have managed to alter hypothesis-testing behaviour. Even so, the evidence of Gorman and Gorman (1984) would appear to provide support for the motivational position—until that is, one examines their procedure closely. In fact the instructions which Gorman and Gorman gave to the "disconfirmation" group where specifically *to test negative predictions*. In other words subjects were instructed not with a general strategy of disconfirmation, but with the specific method that would achieve disconfirmation on the task. The same was true of the instructions given by Tweney et al. (1980) and is probably the reason that they apparently induced disconfirmatory behaviour where the two studies of Mynatt, Doherty, and Tweney had failed.

A great difficulty here is that the motivational view of confirmation bias is so firmly entrenched in the literature that it pervades the terminology used by the experimenters. Thus authors are prone to refer to "confirmatory" and "disconfirmatory" tests (enumerative/eliminative in the original Wason, 1960 paper) when what they are actually describing is whether the subjects made positive or negative tests of their current hypotheses. Similarly, so called "disconfirmatory" instructions which actually instruct subjects to test negative predictions cannot of course distinguish the alternative interpretations of the effects described here.

It is not, then, at all clear from this series of studies that subjects have an anti-Popperian desire to confirm hypotheses which can be corrected by lectures on the philosophy of science. It is, however, clear that people do find it difficult to eliminate hypotheses which form a subset of the actual rule and do not think of testing them in a negative manner unless specifically instructed to do so. The protocols collected by Wason and by Mynatt and Tweney et al. also reveal that subjects can become deeply convinced of an incorrect hypothesis or unable to formulate alternatives when the environment is complex. Before moving on to consideration of the Wason selection task, however, one very interesting finding from this set of studies remains to be discussed.

Tweney et al. (1980), following a suggestion of Wason's, introduced a change of procedure in their fourth experiment which effectively "debiased" their subjects. Subjects were told that the experimenter had two rules in mind, one of which generated "DAX" and the other "MED" triples and that 2 4 6 was an example of a DAX. The DAX rule was in fact the usual "any ascending sequence" and the MED rule any other triple. Hence, the feedback on triples tested was in the form "DAX" and "MED" rather than "right" or "wrong". The result was a dramatic improvement in performance with the majority of subjects announcing the correct rule at the first attempt. This occurred in spite of the fact that the majority of subjects continued to make predominantly "confirmatory" tests of their hypotheses. This finding has been replicated on the "more difficult" 2 4 6 problem by Gorman et al. (1987, Experiment II).

The DAX/MED findings provide clear support for the positivity bias explanation of failures on the 2 4 6 and similar tasks. On the normal task, if the subject forms the hypothesis "ascending with equal intervals is right" then he or she tests repeated positive predictions (triples which conform to this hypothesis) with the usual problems. Logically, the subject has also formed the hypothesis "not ascending with equal intervals is wrong", but they are not aware of this alternate hypothesis and nor are they trying to test it. However, when DAX and MED are substituted for "right" and "wrong", the two hypotheses appear to have equal standing. Subjects succeed *not* because they attempt to disconfirm the DAX hypothesis (as the data of Tweney et al. clearly show) but because they alternately test the MED hypothesis. Because MED is the complement of DAX, a positive test of MED is effectively a negative test of DAX—exactly what is required to eliminate the false hypothesis. Creating a positive label for the negative hypothesis entirely changes subjects' representation of the task. A close parallel to this fascinating finding is provided by Griggs and Newstead's (1982) study of a

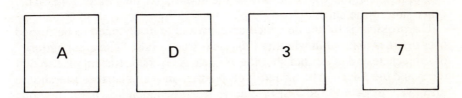

If there is an A on one side of the card then
there is a 3 on the other side of the card

FIG. 3.2.   Example of Wason's selection task.

disjunctive reasoning problem known as THOG (Wason & Brooks, 1979). They found that a problem permitting the use of positive labels to represent a feature of the task normally defined only in an implicit negative manner greatly facilitated reasoning performance. We now consider an alternative and (even) more thoroughly investigated problem invented by Peter Wason, and claimed originally to provide evidence of confirmation bias. The task is sometimes known as the "four card problem" but more commonly as simply the "selection task".

WASON'S SELECTION TASK

Wason (1966) presented a new reasoning problem which has since become one of the most investigated tasks in the history of research into human reasoning. Since research using the Wason selection task relates to a number of main issues in the psychology of reasoning, different aspects of work with this paradigm will be discussed in different chapters of this book. Here we will concentrate upon the task as a model of scientific hypothesis testing and the claim that subjects' errors arise from a form of confirmation bias.

The task is deceptively simple, for in its standard form the great majority of subjects fail to give the correct solution to it. In a typical version of the task the subject will be told that the problem concerns cards which have capital letters on one side and single figure numbers on the other. Sometimes subjects are given a pack of such cards to inspect. They are then shown four cards lying on a table showing two letters and two numbers (for example A,D,3 and 7—see Fig. 3.2). The subject is then told that the experimenter has the following rule in mind which applies to these four cards and may be true or false: "If there is an A on one side of the card, then there is a 3 on the other side of the card."

The problem is to decide which cards would logically need to be turned over in order to find out whether the rule is true or false. The great majority of subjects tested say either that the A card would be sufficient or else that the A and the 3 need to be turned over. Neither answer is correct: one should turn over the A and the 7 or else all four cards depending upon how one interprets the rule. Like the 2 4 6 problem, the four card selection task requires the subject to seek evidence actively rather than simply to evaluate it. The task differs in that the hypothesis to be tested (the rule) is supplied by the experimenter. The subjects can, however, choose to examine evidence which could confirm or disconfirm the rule according to the cards which they specify for turning over. Let us consider each of the cards in turn:

1. The A card. If this were turned over there could either be a number which is a 3 or which is not a 3 on the back. The former would be consistent with the rule but the latter would clearly violate the rule, i.e. show it to be false.
2. The D card. The rule does not specify any condition about letters which are not A's so whatever number is discovered on the back could not disprove the rule.
3. The 3 card. The 3 could have a letter which is an A or which is not an A on the back. Either would be consistent with the rule since it is only required that A's have 3's on the back and not vice versa.
4. The 7 card. If this were turned and there were not an A on the back it would be consistent with the rule. However, if an A were found on the back the card would have an A on one side and a number which is not a 3 on the other, thus violating the rule.

In order to solve this task one needs apparently to appreciate only: (1) that the rule would be false if an A were paired with a number other than 3; and (2) that it is logically necessary to turn over any card which could reveal such a falsifying condition. On this basis clearly the A and the 7 must be chosen while the D and the 3 should not, since whatever they have on the other side cannot disprove the rule. The logical structure is laid out in Fig. 3.3 using a general notation to represent the cards. The rule is taken to be of the general form "If p then q"; p and q represent choices which match the values in the rule (A and 3) whereas not-p and not-q represent "a letter other than A" and

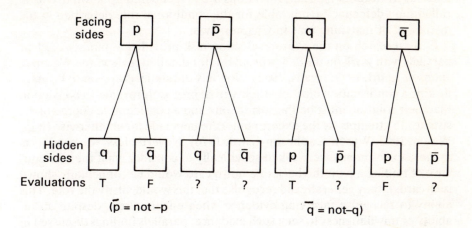

FIG. 3.3.   Logical structure of Wason's selection task for a rule of the form *If p then q*, with evaluations under the defective truth table.

"a number other than 3". Figure 3.3 shows the possible logical combinations by projecting values which might occur on the other sides of the cards together with an evaluation of that combination—T (true), F (false) and ? (irrelevant). Note that the only two cards which can lead to an F at the bottom of the tree are the p and not-q cards (A and 7). The difference between T and ? evaluations is explained below.

Why is the selection task so difficult? One explanation that we should dismiss straight away is that it is due to ambiguity of the rule. Although it says that an A must have a 3 on the back, the subject might well read it to mean that a 3 must also have an A on the back. In this case the subject would be reading the conditional rule as an equivalence rather than an implication. Would that not justify the selection of A and 3? The answer is no. If the rule is taken to read both ways then the correct solution is to choose all four cards which subjects rarely do. The A and 7 must be chosen for the reasons already given. Since it is now assumed that a 3 must have an A on the back, then one must choose 3 and D as well since either could lead to the falsifying combination of a 3 on one side without an A on the other.

Wason's (1966) original explanation was that subjects were exhibiting a verification or confirmation bias. In other words that their error was due to them attempting to find evidence which conforms to the rule rather than that which disconfirms it. We see from Fig. 3.3 that the two cards which can lead to a true (T) evaluation are p and q (A and 3)—the common pattern of choices. This is because any combination containing a not-p has been evaluated as irrelevant (?). The evaluations are in fact based upon what Wason called the "defective" truth table for the conditional rule described in the discussion of matching bias in Chapter Two.

Early research on the Wason selection task provided a number of clear parallels with work on the 2 4 6 problem (for detailed reviews see Wason & Johnson-Laird, 1972; Evans, 1982). Not only did subjects appear to be manifesting a confirmation bias, but their verbal protocols revealed a conviction that their solution must be the correct one and a considerable degree of resistance to attempts by the experimenters to persuade them otherwise (e.g., Wason, 1969; Wason & Johnson-Laird, 1970). Nevertheless, when subjects in these experiments were asked specifically to consider what the consequence of finding a p on the back of a not-q card would be (or actually shown such cards), they generally did recognise that this would falsify the rule. This ability to recognise falsifying evidence when encountered, despite an inability or unwillingness to seek such evidence, parallels findings discussed in the last section, e.g. those of Mynatt et al. (1977).

Several models were proposed to explain errors of reasoning on the selection task, most notably that of Johnson-Laird and Wason (1970a), who proposed that subjects were in one of three states of "insight". Subjects whose choices were determined only by an erroneous verification principle were deemed to have No Insight. Subjects who work only on a falsification principle have Full Insight, whereas those using both principles were classified as having Partial Insight. The choice associated with Partial Insight in the model was that of p, q and not-q. Although this latter combination is rare on the standard task, this choice does occur quite often in experiments designed to increase insight into the need to select the not-q card.

In discussing research on the 2 4 6 problem, I suggested that the confirmation bias manifest in subjects' choices was not due to the subjects attempting to verify their hypotheses, but rather due to an inability to formulate negative tests. In the case of the selection task, strong evidence that the focus on p and q is due to problems with negativity rather than verification bias as such was first presented by Evans and Lynch (1973). To understand their experiment we first need to define the logical status of the four cards in the selection task. These are conventionally referred to as True Antecedent (TA), False Antecedent (FA), True Consequent (TC) and False Consequent (FC). On the affirmative rule these correspond to the p, not-p, q and not-q cards. However, on a rule such as "If p then not q", of course, the negative consequent reverses the correspondence between negations in the instance and the logical status such that TC is now represented by not-q and FC by q, and so on. Evans and Lynch (1973) presented selection tasks in a within subject design such that each subject attempted four problems based on each of the four conditional rules produced by varying the presence of negatives in both antecedent and consequent. If, as was originally believed, subjects are choosing according to a verification bias then they should choose TA and TC, throughout. On the other hand, if matching bias is operating then each logical case should be consistently favoured on the rules where it corresponds to a matching choice (p or q) rather than a mismatching choice (not-p or not-q). The latter prediction was strongly confirmed for all four logical cases in the Evans and Lynch experiment.

As an example, suppose you are shown the same four cards in Fig. 3.2 but asked to test the rule: "If there is an A on one side of the card, then there is not a 3 on the other side of the card." If subjects are attempting to verify the rule then they should now choose the A and the 7, since the combination which conforms to the rule is now an A together with a number other than a 3. On the other hand, if subjects are matching, they should continue to choose A and 3 which in this case is the logically correct choice since the rule is falsified when A and 3 appear on the same card. In fact, when the rule is presented in this general form—*If p then not q*—most subjects choose the matching cards p and q and thus apparently solve the problem.

In the literature on conditional truth tables discussed in Chapter Two, it was observed that "logical" tendency co-existed with matching bias, namely to regard TT as true—and to a lesser extent TF as false—across the four types of rules. Studies investigating negative conditionals on the selection task, following Evans and Lynch, have similarly found a consistent preference for TA and avoidance of FA across the four rules. This is entirely consistent with the hypothesis put forward in the last chapter that two forms of linguistic presupposition are operative in determining the locus of subjects' attention. Whereas matching bias arises from *not* focusing attention on the item it negates, *if* has the effect of directing attention to the hypothesis it proposes (TA rather than FA).

What, though, of the evidence for verification bias? This can be tested for with matching bias controlled by comparing the relative preference between TC and FC over the four rules combined. Evans and Lynch actually found a preference for FC in line with a falsification rather than verification tendency. However, replication studies have been inconsistent in this respect. For example, Manktelow and Evans (1979) found no overall preference between TC and FC in several experiments, whereas other authors have reported a preference for TC (e.g., Reich & Ruth, 1982; Krauth, 1982). All the replications have, however, found consistent and strong evidence of the matching bias effect on the selection task. A recent paper by Beattie and Baron (1988), using an interesting variation on the standard selection task, has claimed strong evidence for both confirmation and matching bias.

In Chapter Two, it was argued that matching bias was due to linguistic suppositions directing attention to matching values and causing their selective encoding. This analysis clearly fits the explanation of matching effects on the selection task also and Evans (1984a) has gone so far as to argue subjects' choices are purely heuristic, i.e. based only on the facing sides of the cards with no logical analysis of what the hidden sides may be. These conclusions are, however, restricted to versions of the selection task using abstract or artificial problem content. The effects of realistic content on this task will be discussed in the next chapter.

Wason and most other authors have generally abandoned the verification bias explanation of abstract selection task performance in the light of the matching bias evidence, but retained the view that 2 4 6 performance reflects a confirmation bias. Yet it should be readily apparent that the positivity bias alternative put forward in this chapter to explain behaviour on the 2 4 6 and related problems is highly similar in nature, to the extent that matching could be considered an example of a more general positivity bias. Specifically, I propose on each task that subjects attempting to test hypotheses think about only some possibilities but not others, the selections being determined by preconscious heuristic processes rather than by logical analysis. Thus they think only of positive consequences or predictions on the 2 4 6 problem and only of investigating the positively named items on the selection task. In both cases, reasoning errors arise from a difficulty in generating the correct features for consideration rather than in a faulty analytic grasp of the logical relationships involved. Hence, on both tasks if subjects are presented with—or happen upon—evidence that logically falsifies the hypothesis under consideration, they will generally recognise this immediately.

Whilst discussion of the effects of realistic content on the selection task is generally deferred to the next chapter, it is pertinent to discuss a couple of relevant papers which are concerned with an attempt to revive the confirmation bias hypothesis in a different form. Van Duyne (1976) introduced some interesting procedural changes. Subjects were asked to generate their own conditional sentences. They were asked to write down five sentences which they considered to be always true and five which they considered sometimes true. Van Duyne termed these necessity and contingency sentences respectively. The experimenter then chose one example of each and administered a task logically equivalent to the selection task, although it did not involve cards. For example if the rule was "If it is a tomato then it is red" the subject would be asked to consider an object which was a tomato but the colour of which was not specified, and asked whether he or she would need more information to test whether the rule was true or false (and so on for each of the four logical cases).

Van Duyne claimed that more correct selections were given with contingency than necessity selections from which he inferred that subjects are more likely to attempt to falsify a rule which they think to be not necessarily true. He proposed the principle of "cognitive self-reinforcement" to explain these findings, which is a subtle form of confirmation bias. Subjects try to confirm the rule if they are convinced it is true, but may try to disconfirm it if they think it may be false. In other words people try to confirm their prior belief in a statement, be it pro or con.

Pollard and Evans (1981) noted that Van Duyne had classified responses as correct only if subjects chose the right cards and in addition stated the correct reason for the choice. This procedure is doubtful in view of the claim of Wason and Evans (1975) that such verbal statements may not reflect the process of reasoning (see Chapter Five). In a re-analysis of Van Duyne's data, Pollard and Evans (1981) showed that there was no effect of conditions on the frequency of card selections when verbal explanations were ignored. However, they repeated Van Duyne's experiment with a stronger manipulation, adding "always false" and "usually false" conditions to the "usually true" and "always true" conditions that were roughly equivalent to those used by Van Duyne. Pollard and Evans in fact found that false sentences were associated with significantly more correct card selections as well as more logical justifications in separate analyses.

The findings of Pollard and Evans (1981) would appear to support Van Duyne's cognitive self-reinforcement principle, although they preferred another explanation of the results based upon availability and associations which I will not go into here. More serious doubt is occasioned by a recent unpublished study by Pollard and Evans which failed to replicate the effect using the standard Wason selection task paradigm with sentences rated *a priori* as believable and unbelievable. The question of how prior beliefs influence reasoning on a number of other tasks will, however, be considered in detail in Chapter Four.

Finally, Johnson-Laird and Wason (1970b) introduced a variant on the selection task in which subjects had only to concentrate on the relevance of the consequent cases q and not-q, and in which they sampled evidence, with feedback, in a sequence of trials. In one experiment subjects were given a rule such as "All the triangles are black" purporting to describe the contents of two boxes, one containing black figures and the other white. The subjects were invited to draw a figure from each box on a series of trials to examine its shape. Logically, the black box (q) is irrelevant but the white box (not-q) needs to be sampled exhaustively in case of a counter-example to the rule, i.e. a white triangle.

This task proved to be much simpler than the standard selection task with all subjects exhausting the contents of the white but not the black box. The number of black shapes unnecessarily requested was taken as the measure of insight. On this index subjects instructed to prove the rule false performed significantly and quite considerably better than those instructed to prove it true. These findings confirm those from some studies of the 2 4 6 type problems discussed earlier in showing (a) that people can apparently exhibit falsifying strategies when the tasks are simplified and (b) that disconfirmatory instructions can sometimes be effective. The reasons for the extra ease of this task and attempts to introduce extra complexity have been explored in a second experiment by Johnson-Laird and Wason (1970b) and in two recent studies (Wason & Green, 1984; Oakhill & Johnson-Laird, 1985a).

In summary, the Wason selection task, like the 2 4 6 problem, produces strong evidence of cognitive failure on a task which involves active hypothesis testing—laboratory simulations of the process involved in scientific reasoning. In my view, in neither case is the evidence for a confirmation bias, in the sense of a motivation to verify rather than falsify hypotheses, very well founded. What each demonstrates very clearly, however, is that people may fail to find falsifying evidence due to a tendency to focus on positive information. The final set of studies to be considered in this chapter concern evidence from a different type of task, involving statistical reasoning, which has also been claimed as evidence for confirmation bias.

DIAGNOSTICITY AND PSEUDO-DIAGNOSTICITY

Evidence for confirmation bias in the testing of statistical hypotheses has been claimed by Doherty, Mynatt, Tweney, and Schiavo (1979). In discussion of the base rate fallacy in Chapter Two, it was indicated that Bayes' theorem provides that the posterior odds between rival hypotheses are equal to the product of the prior odds and the likelihood ratio. If the hypotheses are designated as H1 and H2 and the evidence as D this can be stated formally by the following equation:

$$\frac{P(H1/D)}{P(H2/D)} = \frac{P(H1)}{P(H2)} \times \frac{P(D/H1)}{P(D/H2)}$$

For those unfamiliar with the notation, P designates the probability of the event within the following parentheses and the / sign indicates conditional probability. Thus $P(H1/D)$ should be read as "the probability of H1, given the observation of D". The term "odds" is used to designate the ratio between two probabilities. The left hand side of the equation, the posterior odds, thus designates the relative likelihood of the two hypotheses after observation of the datum D. The prior odds are the ratio of the probabilities of the two hypotheses—$P(H1)$, $P(H2)$—before observing D. The likelihood ratio is the relative likelihood of D given the assumption that either hypothesis is true.

The evidence that people violate this normative decision rule by ignoring the prior odds or base rate in favour of exclusive interest in the immediate evidence, D, has already been discussed in Chapter Two. Here we are concerned instead with people's understanding of the two probabilities $P(D/H1)$ and $P(D/H2)$. The datum D is said to be *diagnostic* if the likelihood ratio deviates from 1, i.e. if it provides better evidence for one hypothesis than the other. It is, however, important to realise that diagnosticity depends solely on the ratio of the two likelihoods and not their absolute values.

Suppose, for example, you were a doctor trying to decide whether a patient was suffering from a particular disease(H1) or not (H2) and that you knew that the patient had a positive result on a given medical test (D). Knowing that, say, 80% of sufferers of this disease yielded a positive result on the test ($P(D/H1)$) would be meaningless in itself without knowing the likelihood of a positive result in non-sufferers ($P(D/H2)$). If the latter probability were also 80% then the test would obviously be entirely non-diagnostic and useless. If non-sufferers were only 10% likely to produce a positive test then the likelihood ratio would be 8 to 1 in favour of the hypothesis that the disease was present, and so on. The relevance of prior odds to this decision can also be seen. Even if the likelihood ratio following the test result was strongly in favour of the disease—say 100 to 1—this evidence should still be disregarded if the disease is very rare. For example, if the prior odds were 10,000 to 1 against a patient of this type having the disease then the posterior odds would still be 100 to 1 against following the test.

Doherty et al. (1979) devised a task to test the adequacy of subjects' understanding of diagnosticity of evidence. As in the other tasks discussed in this chapter subjects were permitted to choose which evidence to sample in order to test their hypotheses. They were given a scenario in which they had to imagine that they were undersea explorers who had discovered a pot and wished to return it to its homeland—one of two islands. Subjects were provided with a description of six characteristics of the pot, for example, whether the clay was smooth or rough and whether or not it had handles. Subjects were then permitted to seek six pieces of information from a possible twelve pieces. The information concerned the probability of each characteristic being present in pots from either island.

Each of the features is a datum (D1 ... D6). In order to gain diagnostic evidence relevant to the decision, subjects should choose to discover three pairs of probabilities, so that they know for three of the features their relative likelihood of being found on either island. The analysis showed, however, that a large number of subjects formed a favoured hypothesis about a particular island at the outset and then sampled mostly or exclusively evidence about that island ($P(D1/H1)$, $P(D2,H1)$ etc.) ignoring the other. Doherty et al. (1979) regarded this as evidence for confirmation bias and referred to the fallacious belief that absolute probabilities of the $P(D/H)$ type were relevant as "pseudo-diagnosticity".

Once again we might ask whether subjects' bias to gather evidence relevant to the favoured hypothesis is a confirmation bias in a motivational sense or a cognitive failure, in this case due to failure to understand the concept of diagnosticity. A study by Beyth-Marom and Fischhoff (1983) is relevant. In their first experiment subjects were given a scenario commencing as follows: "You have met Mr. Maxwell at a party to which only university professors and business executives were invited. The only thing you know about Mr. Maxwell is that he is a member of the Bear's Club." At this point instructions diverged, with one group being asked to assess the probability that Mr. Maxwell was a university professor, and the other to decide whether it was more probable that he was a university professor than a business executive. Although the question does not affect the logic of the task, the former, asymmetric form might be expected to induce a confirmation bias, by focusing subjects' attention on one alternative.

Beyth-Marom and Fischhoff's subjects were asked to rate the relevance of several questions which they could ask to get further information relevant to their decision. The interest was in their ratings of questions concerning the two probabilities $P(D/H1)$ and $P(D/H2)$ where H1 is the professor hypothesis, H2 the executive hypothesis, and D is the fact of membership of the Bear's Club. For example, the $P(D/H1)$ question was expressed as "What percentage of the university professors at the party are members of the Bear's Club". While most subjects thought that $P(D/H1)$ was relevant, only 54% of subjects in the asymmetric group judged $P(D/H2)$ relevant, compared with 78% in the symmetric group, which would seem to replicate Doherty et al.'s findings for subjects with a preferred hypothesis.

In another experiment Beyth-Marom and Fischhoff found that the percentage of subjects rating $P(D/H2)$ as relevant dropped from 55% to 35% in a group warned not to seek redundant information, suggesting that people's understanding of the need for this information is fairly tenuous. People's misunderstanding of diagnosticity was further confirmed in an experiment which showed that the majority of those subjects who regarded $P(D/H2)$ as relevant did so for the wrong reason! The final experiment in this paper showed, however, that when subjects were presented with evidence concerning both $P(D/H1)$ and $P(D/H2)$, they did take account of the latter in a correct way when assessing the posterior odds, providing apparently contradictory evidence that people do have some understanding of diagnosticity. In their conclusions, Beyth-Marom and Fischhoff emphasise, not confirmation bias as such, but rather people's failure to select and organise relevant information for themselves in an appropriate manner. Their conclusion is quite compatible with my analysis of the causes of bias on the 2 4 6 and selection task problems.

CONCLUSIONS

The work on diagnosticity and pseudo-diagnosticity, whilst dealing with statistical decision making, produces comparable findings to those on the other inductive and deductive reasoning tasks reviewed in this chapter. That is, subjects tend to focus on a particular hypothesis and show rather poor understanding of the best strategies for testing it, often with the consequence that they fail to eliminate an incorrect hypothesis. In general, however, subjects seem much better at making use of relevant information which is presented to them than at devising appropriate strategies to discover such evidence.

The review given here is inevitably selective and has been focused on reasoning research in the "cognitive" tradition. It should be noted at this point that there is a considerable body of work conducted by social psychologists which could be deemed relevant to the issue of confirmation bias. For example, Nisbett and Ross (1980, Chapter Eight) review a number of studies which have shown that social beliefs and theories, once acquired, are frequently maintained in the light of conflicting evidence. There are also claims that people show confirmation bias in the way in which they go about testing social hypotheses (see, for example, Darley & Gross, 1983).

On the basis of the literatures reviewed here, however, I am tempted to claim that "confirmation bias" is somewhat mythical. The studies do show confirmatory behaviour, but have not clearly demonstrated the existence of confirmatory intentions. Just as an apparent verification bias on the Wason selection task is now generally accepted to be a by-product of matching bias, I wish to claim that the demonstrable deficiencies in the way in which people go about testing and eliminating hypotheses are a function of selective processing induced by a widespread cognitive difficulty in thinking about any information which is essentially negative in its conception.

A recent discussion of confirmation bias by Klayman and Ha (1987) is similar in some respects to the interpretation offered here. They also argue that errors on the 2 4 6 and similar problems reflect positive testing and that this only leads to confirmation because of the relation between the subject's and experimenter's hypothesis that obtains on this particular type of task (cf. Fig. 3.1). On the basis of a discussion of a wide range of hypothesis testing tasks they suggest that people adopt a general default heuristic which they term a "positive test strategy" and argue that this is often appropriate and effective when applied to tasks of different structures. Whilst I agree with a number of their arguments and conclusions, the view proposed here differs in subtle but significant ways. In essence, whereas Klayman and Ha attribute positive testing to a "strategy" learned in one situation and misapplied in another, I regard what I term positivity bias as reflecting the operation of pre-attentive processes which direct attention to positive rather than negative information. Hence, I link the bias to the difficulties in understanding linguistic and logical negation outside of hypothesis testing situations. I also regard it as one type of "heuristic" process (in the Evans, 1984a sense) which may combine with others in determining attention. For example, it was argued in the discussion of the Wason selection task earlier in this chapter that selections on the abstract version of the problem reflect the combined influence of linguistic presuppositions arising from *if,* and *not* on the perceived relevance of the cards.

Perhaps what this chapter has shown most clearly is that (a) it is relatively simple to demonstrate clear and replicable evidence of bias and error in human reasoning, but that (b) it is most difficult to achieve a consensus on the interpretation of the phenomena observed. In my experience these two conclusions are by no means confined to the study of confirmation bias but hold across the entire range of reasoning research. From a practical point of view, however, the existence of the reasoning errors discussed in this chapter, and the results of attempts to debiase them, are of considerable importance regardless of the theoretical interpretation which you prefer.

4 Effects of Content and Context

An important distinction which may be made for any reasoning problem is that between its *form* and its *content*. Conventionally, the form of a problem is analysed in terms of its logical structure, so that it is seen to be a test of people's understanding of conditional logic, the law of large numbers, or whatever. We have seen in the previous two chapters a number of examples of how subjects' apparent competence in reasoning with a given principle varies considerably between and across different experiments depending on the manipulation of a number of variables independent of the logical form of the problems. These are mostly what I would term *presentation* variables, including such manipulations as the complexity of problem wording, the relationship of linguistic and logical variables, and the presence of various instructional sets.

Most of the experiments discussed to date have not, however, explicitly manipulated the problem content in the sense to be discussed in this chapter. By content, I refer to the nature of the scenario or context in which the problem is placed and the specific meaning of the propositions or other elements linked in the logical structure. For example, in a study of reasoning with conditional sentences of the form *If p then q* a content manipulation would concern the nature of the propositions substituted for p and q and the context for the sentence created by the instructions. At least three general types of problem content can be distinguished: (1) abstract content; (2) arbitrarily realistic content; and (3) knowledge-related content. An example of the first category would be the use of artificial letter-number rules in several of the experiments on conditional reasoning, including most of those demonstrating the "matching bias" effect. The second category uses problem content phrased in everyday terms but lacking any direct connection with knowledge or beliefs that the subject might bring to bear in solving the problem. Examples of the use of realistic, but still arbitrary problem content have been encountered in some of the examples of statistical reasoning discussed to date, such as the blue and green cabs and the maternity hospital problem. In these cases it is unlikely that subjects will have any direct experience or beliefs about the domains in which these problems are set which could influence their understanding of the principle being tested.

In this chapter, I will be discussing research on human reasoning in which the content of problems is varied as the principal manipulation of interest while factors affecting form and presentation are held constant (or manipulated independently). Some such studies have compared abstract with arbitrarily realistic content, but the major interest has been with problem contents which invoke prior knowledge of (psychological) relevance to the logical task. For some reason, the great majority of such studies have involved deductive rather than inductive or statistical reasoning. Hence, the major sections of this chapter focus exclusively on the topic with regard to deductive reasoning. I have, however, included a section late in the chapter which discusses the limited amount of relevant work on statistical inference and relates these studies to the general issues discussed throughout the chapter.

The study of content factors in reasoning is effectively the study of the relationship between knowledge and inference. This is theoretically critical whether the focus of interest is on the mechanisms underlying reasoning competence, or on the causes of errors and biases. Clearly, the strength and multiplicity of the content effects which have emerged in the experimental literature have to be explained by either the competence or performance component of a theory of reasoning mechanisms. At the same time, content factors are critical in the discussion of bias. For example, some authors have claimed that the use of meaningful, realistic content effectively removes biases observed in abstract or arbitrary versions of reasoning problems. If this were so, then the evidence of error in the psychological literature might present a misleading and unnecessarily anxiety-provoking picture of real life and expert reasoning as some authors have suggested (e.g., Cohen, 1981). On the other hand, prior knowledge is claimed in a number of studies to introduce new sources of bias and error.

In this chapter, I will examine evidence claimed both for the biasing and debiasing effects of problem content which evokes prior knowledge. First, however, I will discuss some general theoretical issues concerning the relationship between knowledge and reasoning.

KNOWLEDGE AND REASONING

A distinction commonly made in cognitive science is that between *declarative* and *procedural* knowledge. Whilst the former term refers to knowledge of facts, concepts, and relationships, all of which can be stated in verbal or propositional form, the latter refers to knowledge of how to do things. For example, a psychology student is acquiring declarative knowledge when learning the details of published theories and experiments for description in an examination, but acquiring procedural knowledge when learning how to design well-controlled experiments and to perform statistical analyses. In computer software, declarative knowledge might be a set of facts held in a database whereas procedural knowledge would consist of rules, heuristics, or algorithms capable of processing such data.

The ability to reason is clearly a form of procedural knowledge. On the basis of a set of premises, assumptions, or observations (declarative knowledge) an individual generates an inductive or deductive inference. There is, however, considerable disagreement amongst psychologists about the form of the procedural knowledge which underlies such inferences. As indicated in Chapter One, the major theoretical approaches are of three types: (1) general purpose inference rules or heuristics; (2) pragmatic reasoning schemas; and (3) mental models. The first two approaches are primarily distinguished by the level of abstraction at which they propose rules and heuristics to be held, whilst the mental models approach as espoused by Johnson-Laird (1983) denies the existence of inference rules at any level of abstraction and proposes instead that reasoning reflects only a strategy of searching for counter-examples amongst semantic representations. The term "mental models" is, however, widely and variously used and rule-based versions have been proposed by other authors (e.g., Holland, Holyoak, Nisbett, & Thagard, 1986).

The study of content effects in reasoning can be viewed as an investigation of the relationship between declarative and procedural knowledge in human cognition. The traditional perspective is that memory (equated with declarative knowledge) and reasoning are essentially separate systems. According to this view, humans have what Johnson-Laird (1983) calls a "mental logic" in the form of internalised logical procedures or natural inference rules (e.g., Inhelder & Piaget, 1958; Henle, 1962; Braine, 1978; Rips, 1983). This approach assumes that people possess a set of highly abstract reasoning schemas which can be applied to any problem of a given logical structure.

Clearly, the existence of content effects in reasoning provides a problem for such theories which has been rather scantily addressed by proponents of this approach. In particular, such theories are seriously incomplete in that they fail to describe the necessary encoding and decoding stages that must precede and follow reasoning. That is to say, in order for the inference rules to be employed, the content of a given problem must first be encoded into an abstract representation to which the rules can be applied. The subsequent inferences must then be decoded back into the terms of the original domain. Whilst Rips (1983) has at least provided a specific theory of the central stage—the application of rules to generate inferences—no-one has proposed specific mechanisms for encoding and decoding—i.e. translation between domain-dependent and abstract levels of representation.

It seems to me that in order to account for content effects an inference rule theory must: (1) propose that syntactically equivalent propositions are encoded into differing abstract representations according to their content and context; and (2) include additional inference rules to accommodate these different representations. For example, consider the case of how conditional reasoning is affected by the nature of the content in the antecedent and consequent propositions.

In a series of experiments, Fillenbaum (1975; 1976; 1978) has investigated the effects of context on conditional inferences. In particular he investigated the inverse (or denial of the antecedent) inference. Consider the following two examples:

E1:   If it is a cat then it is an animal;
       It is not a cat;
       Therefore, it is not an animal.

E2:   If you mow the lawn I will give you five dollars;
       You do not mow the lawn;
       Therefore, I will not give you five dollars.

E1 is an example of what is called a contingent universal, while E2 is a promise. The reader's intuitions will doubtless confirm Fillenbaum's findings. Few subjects endorse E1 as a valid inference, though many would agree that the conclusion of E2 is sound. The logical form of the two arguments is, of course, identical. The difference lies in the prior knowledge we bring to bear. When threats or promises are used, the speaker normally intends a biconditional or equivalence interpretation of the statement. Quite simply, it makes no sense to promise a reward contingent upon an action, if you intend to deliver the reward anyway. To do so would violate Grice's (1975) maxims of conversational implicatures—not to speak of common sense!

Other authors have shown that more generally, the use of temporal-causal contexts increases the likelihood that subjects will reason as though the statement *If p then q* implied its converse *If q then p* e.g., Staudenmayer, 1975; Marcus & Rips, 1979). A recent study of reasoning with realistic disjunctive statements has shown analogous contextual dependency effects (Newstead, Griggs, & Chrostowski, 1984). The solution for an inference rule theory would appear to be to assume that there is a one-to-many mapping between the syntactic form of the statements in the problem domain and their abstract representations. Hence, according to context the conditional is encoded in differing ways. For example, Rips (1983) has suggested that his theory would have to be extended in this way to account for reasoning with causal conditionals.

One problem that arises here is that the apparent parsimony of the inference rule approach is severely compromised once one realises that very sophisticated encoding and decoding mechanisms are required to make it work. Also, a number of content effects are much more complex than so far indicated. Although it is moot whether the DA inference induced by E2 above is an error, the content effects to be discussed in the next section very definitely constitute biases. Moreover, I would argue that the kinds of biases involved cannot plausibly be explained by the application of any kind of inference rule—however defective.

The theory of pragmatic reasoning schemas by its very nature deals with the relationship between knowledge and reasoning head on, in that the schemas elicited by the context of the problem include domain-sensitive knowledge of both the declarative and procedural variety. Hence, embedded within the schema are rules and heuristics which are derived from experience in the domain and whose application is similarly limited (see, for example, Rumelhart, 1980). The role of schema theory will be discussed later in the chapter since it has been one of the main motivators of recent research into the debiasing effects of problem content. The theory of reasoning by mental models also permits, in principle, the reasoner to construct models, the nature of which is influenced by prior knowledge of the domain as well as the specific information presented in the problem. The theory has been applied to the explanation of both biasing and debiasing effects of problem content (see Johnson-Laird, 1983; Oakhill & Johnson-Laird, 1985b).

The understanding of content effects is important for practical and applied reasons as well as for the kinds of theoretical reasons discussed above. Cognitive science has an important area of application known as cognitive or knowledge engineering. Here, the concern is particularly with the elicitation of knowledge from human experts and the simulation of their reasoning in "expert system" computer programs (see, for example, Hayes-Roth, Waterman, & Lenat, 1983). I have argued elsewhere (Evans, 1988) that the theory and methodology of cognitive psychology has much to offer generally to the problem of knowledge elicitation. Psychological understanding of expert reasoning may also lead to suggestions for improvements in the kinds of inferencing mechanisms that are implemented in expert systems and other kinds of A I programs. The specific point of relevance here is that expert reasoning is, by definition, carried out in the context of detailed knowledge and experience of the domain in question.

Whilst I do not believe it is necesary to study only "expert" subjects in the sense that the layman would use the term, it clearly is important to study knowledge-based reasoning in order to make reasonable extrapolations of practical value to this area. It is also very important to understand the nature of any biases which may affect expert reasoning since we would clearly wish to avoid the accidental introduction of these into expert systems through the knowledge elicitation process (cf. Evans, 1987a; 1988). In the remainder of this chapter I will examine the evidence for both biasing and debiasing effects of knowledge on reasoning and consider theoretical explanations for these effects.

BIASING EFFECTS OF KNOWLEDGE

Belief Bias in Deductive Reasoning

The principal phenomenon to be discussed here is that of the so-called "belief bias" effect in deductive reasoning which has been investigated mostly on tasks incorporating classical Aristotelian syllogistic logic. Before defining and discussing the effect, a little background on the nature of deductive reasoning tasks and work on syllogistic reasoning is necessary.

In a deductive reasoning task subjects are usually instructed to make a *validity* judgement: that is to say they must decide whether or not a conclusion follows logically from the premises stated. By definition, a deductive inference rests upon the assumptions stated and no other knowledge or belief is relevant. The logical validity of an argument should be judged purely on the syntactic structure of the premises and conclusion and is entirely independent of the meaning of the propositions concerned. Experimental instructions are normally worded in an attempt to indicate as clearly as possible that a validity judgement is required. For example, Evans, Barston, and Pollard (1983 p.298, Experiment 1) presented subjects with syllogisms embedded in prose passages and instructed their subjects as follows:

> This is an experiment to test people's reasoning ability. You will be given four
> problems. In each case you will be given a prose passage to read and asked if
> certain conclusions may be logically deduced from it. You should answer this
> question on the assumption that all the information given in the passage is, in
> fact, true. If you judge that a conclusion necessarily follows from the state-
> ments in the passage then you should answer "yes", otherwise "no".

Note that the term "validity"—which is not generally understood by naive subjects in its logical sense—is not included in these instructions. The wording is, however, intended to convey the underlying concept: the truth of the conclusion is judged on the basis of the assumed truth of the premises, and the conclusion should only be approved if it *necessarily* follows. Whether instructions of this type adequately convey the required concept is, however, moot as we shall see.

Now, when a subject is presented with a deductive argument, with instructions such as these, the question which first arises is whether he or she has the logical competence to assess validity. Most of the experiments to be discussed in this section concern reasoning with classical syllogisms, examples of which are shown in Table 4.1. A considerable amount of research has been carried out into syllogistic reasoning using materials that are either artificial (All As are Bs) or arbitrarily realistic (All artists are beekeepers). A detailed review of such research by Evans (1982, Chapter Six) provided a rather negative picture: (1) subjects make many judgements which are in conflict with a logical analysis—in particular they often endorse invalid conclusions, i.e. those which are not determined by their premises; and (2) subjects are systematically biased in their judgements by the syntactic structure of the syllogisms. The principal biases claimed are those of "atmosphere" and "figural bias" which I do not have space to describe here. It should be noted, however, that the status of the former is particularly disputed with some authors preferring to attribute the logical errors concerned to misrepresentation of the premises (e.g., Chapman & Chapman, 1959; Revlis 1975a; 1975b). Such authors argue that the process of reasoning itself is fairly logical. Explanations of both types of biases have also been offered within the theory that syllogistic reasoning involves the manipulation of mental models (cf. Johnson-Laird & Steedman, 1978; Johnson-Laird & Bara, 1984).

Realistic content was, however, introduced into syllogistic reasoning experiments in one of the earliest reported studies (Wilkins, 1928). Her findings led to two hypotheses: (1) that realistic content can facilitate logical reasoning relative to artificial problem content; and (2) that the existence of prior beliefs and attitudes can bias reasoning. The former hypotheses will be discussed in the later part of this chapter. The latter—the belief bias—hypotheses, can now be explained. In essence, the problem arises when subjects have prior beliefs about the conclusion of the argument. Belief bias is exhibited when subjects reject a logically valid conclusion which is unbelievable or when they accept an invalid conclusion which is believable. In other words, it appears that subjects are ignoring the instructions and basing their assessment of the conclusion on prior knowledge and belief rather than on the premises presented.

Following Wilkins (1928) a number of papers have been published at intervals claiming to replicate the belief bias effect. However, most of the studies in the literature prior to 1980 have been subjected to various criticisms in terms of the methodology employed (cf. Pollard, 1979; Evans, 1982; Barston, 1986; Revlin, Leirer, Yopp, & Yopp, 1980). Recent interest in the belief bias effect stems from the paper of Revlin et al. (1980). Having seriously questioned the existence of the effect by criticism of the earlier literature, they reported experiments of their own with tighter controls in which a significant belief bias was nevertheless observed. However, Revlin et al. claimed the effect to be very weak compared with the effects of logic on their subjects' performance and suggested that belief bias was not a major influence in deductive reasoning.

Evans et al. (1983), however, pointed to a number of features in the design of Revlin et al.'s experiments which may have led them to underestimate the size of the effect. Some of the problems arose from their use of a paradigm in which the subject had to choose a conclusion from a list of alternatives. Evans et al. reported three experiments of their own using a simpler methodology in which subjects are presented with the two premises of the argument together with a conclusion and asked to make a yes/no judgement on whether the conclusion necessarily follows (see instructions quoted above). The logical form of the syllogisms was chosen so as to avoid the principal criticisms made by Revlin et al. of earlier studies.

The Evans et al. problems were divided into four basic categories depending upon whether or not the conclusion was valid—i.e. logically determined by the premises—and whether or not the conclusion was *a priori* believable. Believability was measured by a rating task given to a separate group of subjects drawn from the same population. Examples of syllogisms of the four types, Valid-Believable, Valid-Unbelievable, Invalid-Believable and Invalid-Unbelievable, are shown in Table 4.1. Over the three experiments, several other factors were varied including the presence or absence of a prose passage surrounding the premises and the use of various verbalisation

TABLE 4.1
Examples of the Four Types of Syllogism Used By
Evans, Barston, and Pollard (1983)

Valid-believable
No police dogs are vicious
Some highly trained dogs are vicious

Therefore, some highly trained dogs are not police dogs

Valid-unbelievable
No nutritional things are inexpensive
Some vitamin tablets are inexpensive

Therefore, some vitamin tablets are not nutritional

Invalid-believable
No addictive things are inexpensive
Some cigarettes are inexpensive

Therefore, some addictive things are not cigarettes

Invalid-unbelievable
No millionaires are hard workers
Some rich people are hard workers

Therefore, some millionaires are not rich people

procedures discussed later. However, the basic pattern of responding to the four problem types was consistent across these manipulations and the aggregate data of the three experiments is shown in Table 4.2.

As is obvious from Table 4.2 three clear (and consistently significant) findings emerged. "Yes" decisions—conclusions accepted—were made far more often on valid than invalid problems in line with the logic of the syllogism. There was, however, an equally strong tendency overall for believable conclusions to be accepted more often than unbelievable ones—providing strong evidence of a *substantial* belief bias effect. There was also a consistently significant interaction between the two factors. One way of expressing this interaction is to say that logical validity had more effect on unbelievable than believable conclusions. Alternatively, it could be stated that the belief bias effect is more marked for invalid than valid arguments. Which of these two interpretations is the more appropriate depends upon which of two models of the belief bias effect is preferred (discussed later).

Evans et al. also conducted a number of protocol analyses, mostly based on concurrent "think aloud" protocols (see Chapter Five for general discussion of this methodology). One of these analyses involved scoring the presence and absence of mentions of the premises and of irrelevant information. A strong correlation was found between the protocol scores and decisions made. For example, on Valid Unbelievable problems—where logic and belief conflict—subjects making (logical) "yes" decisions made significantly more references to the premises and fewer to irrelevant information compared with those making (belief based) "no " decisions. This finding is consistent with the claim of Henle (1962) that errors in reasoning occur when subjects "fail to accept the logical task" and reason on the basis of prior beliefs rather than the premises presented. Alternatively, it may also be that the verbalisations are simply rationalisations of decisions determined by preconscious processes (cf. Wason & Evans, 1975 and Chapter Five of this book). However, against the latter view is the fact that the same pattern was found by Evans et al. in both retrospective and concurrent verbalisation protocols.

TABLE 4.2
Percentage Conclusions Accepted in the Study
of Evans, Barston, and Pollard (1983) Averaged
Over Three Experiments ($N = 120$)

	Believable	Unbelievable
Valid	89	56
Invalid	71	10

The second protocol analysis reported by Evans et al. (1983) produced some very interesting findings. Using only think-aloud protocols from Experiments 2 and 3 they categorised them into three types: C protocols in which subjects referred only to the conclusion of the syllogism; CP protocols in which they referred to the conclusion and *subsequently* to the premises; and PC protocols in which they referred to the premises and then subsequently to the conclusion. C protocols were taken to indicate a conclusion-centred reasoning strategy, PC cases regarded as showing forwards premise-to-conclusion reasoning with the CP type intermediate. When the decision data were analysed separately for each type it emerged that the belief bias effect was most strongly marked for problems on which C protocols were observed and was least strong on PC protocols. The relative frequency of logically correct decisions ran in the opposite direction with PC protocols associated with most and C protocols with fewest.

These analyses are, of course, of a correlational nature but they do suggest a plausible picture of belief bias effects. When subjects focus on the conclusion they tend to exhibit belief bias and bring in extraneous information to support their decisions. Subjects who indicate they are considering the premises are more likely to give logical decisions and less likely to show belief bias, especially if they appear to be reasoning in a premise-to-conclusion direction. This analysis does, however, raise a further interesting question. Is the belief bias effect only observed because a conclusion is presented along with the premises? Would subjects show a tendency to generate more believable conclusions if simply given the premises and asked to state what conclusions followed?

Whilst the method of Evans et al. might be described as an evaluation task, the alternative method is best characterised as a construction task. Barston (1986, Experiments 4 and 5) devised syllogistic construction tasks incorporating similar problem materials to those used by Evans et al. (1983). No evidence was found that the conclusions produced by subjects were more likely to be believable than unbelievable. However, Oakhill and Johnson-Laird (1985b) did find evidence of a belief bias in a syllogistic construction task. On close examination the findings of the two studies are not in conflict. Oakhill and Johnson-Laird found the effect only for materials with *definitionally* true and false conclusions, such as "Some of the actresses are not women" and not for *empirically* true and false conclusions such as "Some of the healthy people are not athletes". Although this factor was not considered in the preparation of Barston's materials, *post hoc* examination reveals that hers were predominantly of the empirical type.

The discrepancy between the syllogistic evaluation task and production task is not surprising since the cognitive demands of the two are very different. As the protocol analyses of Evans et al. suggest, the presence of a conclusion can cause subjects to focus their attention upon it to the relative neglect of the premises — another example of selective processing of the problem content as a cause of bias. It is less clear how subjects proceed on the production task but it must clearly encourage premise-to-conclusion reasoning which weakens the effects of belief bias. When beliefs are particularly strong, however, it may be that possible conclusions spring to mind from the context for evaluation, or that conclusions produced by reasoning are rejected if they appear obviously anomalous.

The following section will concentrate on the explanation of belief bias in the evaluation paradigm. Lest the reader thinks that such a paradigm lacks ecological validity, it is worth mentioning the study of Lord, Ross, and Lepper (1979). They presented their subjects with reports of research studies purporting to find evidence for or against the deterrent effects of capital punishment—an emotive topic on which attitudes were polarised between two experimental groups. The studies subjects evaluated used differing methodologies but these were counterbalanced across subjects so that a given method was used to support subjects' prior beliefs for half the subjects and to provide evidence against it for the other half. The study found clear evidence that subjects were far more critical of whatever methodology happened to be used in the study with the conclusions of which they disagreed. This finding is more characteristic of the belief bias effect discussed in this chapter than the confirmation bias discussed in Chapter Two (though the two are, perhaps, related). Whilst confirmation bias refers to a tendency to seek evidence favouring prior beliefs, belief bias concerns the biased evaluation of evidence according to the believability of the conclusion which it produces.

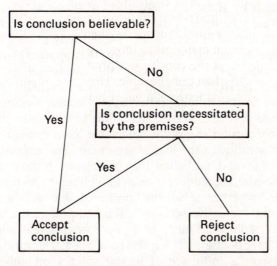

FIG. 4.1.   The Selective Scrutiny model of belief bias (adapted from Barston, 1986).

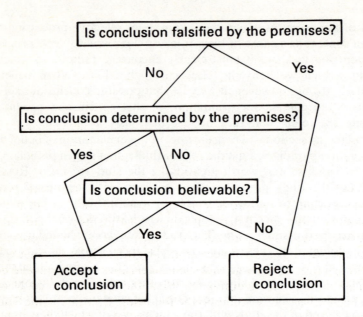

FIG. 4.2. The Misinterpreted Necessity model of belief bias (adapted from Barston, 1986).

Two Models of Belief Bias

Evans et al. (1983) put forward two possible models of belief bias in their attempt to explain the interaction between logic and belief shown in Table 4.2. These were later labelled the Selective Scrutiny and Misinterpreted Necessity models by Barston (1986) and are shown in Figs. 4.1 and 4.2. These models are schematic in the sense that the diagrams show actions as being determinate that in fact can be claimed only to be a dominant tendency. For example, the data do not support the apparent claim of the Selective Scrutiny model in Fig. 4.1 that believable conclusions are invariably accepted, but they do show that such acceptances are highly probable.

The Selective Scrutiny model reflects the conclusion-centred interpretation of belief bias discussed above. According to this model the subject first examines the conclusion and if it is believable has a strong tendency to accept it without scrutiny of the logical argument. This explains the high acceptance rate of invalid but believable conclusions. If the conclusion is unbelievable, however, the subject is much more likely to perform some analysis to determine whether or not the conclusion does follow from the premises—hence the "selective scrutiny". Barston prefers the mental models explanation (cf. Johnson-Laird, 1983) of how this reasoning is actually achieved but I have deliberately left this issue open. This model accounts for the more substantial influence of logical validity on unbelievable conclusions which characterises the interaction shown in Table 4.2.

The Selective Scrutiny model is attractive for a number of reasons. It explains the belief-by-logic interaction whilst maintaining a view of belief bias compatible with the protocol analyses of Evans et al. (1983) and the weaker belief bias effect on the construction task. It also fits well with the "biased assimilation" studies in social psychology such as those of Lord et al. (1979). Selective scrutiny of the methodology of studies with the conclusions of which they disagreed, provides a clear explanation of the behaviour of subjects in that study. However, Evans et al. recognised the existence of a serious rival hypothesis which Barston has termed the Misinterpreted Necessity model.

This model was inspired by the claims of Dickstein (1980; 1981) that subjects misunderstand the nature of logical necessity. In the Evans et al. experiments—as in most syllogistic reasoning experiments—the invalid conclusions were not actually contradicted by the premises. They were *compatible* with the premises but not necessitated by them. If Dickstein is correct, subjects might not understand that such conclusions must be invalid but regard them rather as indeterminate. What the Misinterpreted Necessity model (Fig. 4.2) actually assumes is the following. Contrary to the Selective Scrutiny model it supposes that logical analysis precedes rather than follows belief effects. The subject first attempts to prove the conclusion either determinately true or false on the basis of the premises (the latter is not logically possible with the Evans et al. problems). If both fail then the conclusion is psychologically indeterminate, so the subject falls back on a belief heuristic to make the decision. If the tendencies are as described by this model, then valid conclusions will tend to be accepted with little effect of belief, whereas invalid conclusions will be subject to substantial belief bias effects. Hence, this model provides an alternative explanation of the effect of logic, belief, and the interaction of the two factors.

In order to test the Misinterpreted Necessity model, Barston (1986, Experiments 6–8) conducted a series of experiments on the syllogistic evaluation task in which the nature of instruction given to subjects was manipulated. Standard instructions, similar to those of Evans et al. (1983) were compared with augmented instructions incorporating the explanation of logical necessity used by Dickstein (1981). According to the Misinterpreted Necessity model, augmented instructions should raise the frequency of rejection of invalid conclusions and eliminate the belief-by-logic interaction. The evidence for these predictions was weak. In only one of the three experiments was there a substantial drop in the frequency of acceptance of Valid Unbelievable conclusions and in none was there a significant difference in the extent of the belief-by-logic interaction between the groups given the two differing kinds of instructions.

Evans and Pollard (1987) took a different approach to the problem, by investigating the effects of problem complexity. They argued that increasing the logical difficulty of a deductive argument should have differing effects on belief bias according to the two rival models. Both models will, of course, assume that complexity will increase the overall frequency of logical errors, but only the Misinterpreted Necessity model predicts that complexity will also induce more belief bias. According to this model, belief bias reflects a heuristic on which subjects fall back if they fail to deduce a determinately true or false conclusion by logical analysis. Hence, on complex problems the belief heuristic should operate more often. Under the Selective Scrutiny model, however, belief bias may be expected to be independent of complexity since the believability check *precedes* any logical analysis. If (selective) scrutinisation is made more difficult when it occurs by complex problems, this is assumed to result in random error not related to believability.

Evans and Pollard report two experiments using deductive evaluation tasks based upon conditional logic rather than standard categorical syllogism. In the first experiment the complexity manipulation was based on the nature of the component inferences required. In the second experiment a stronger manipulation was used in which subjects had to reason from four as opposed to two premises. The results of both experiments were similar. In each case a significant effect of conclusion believability was found in line with the belief bias hypothesis. In each experiment the complexity manipulation succeeded in reducing subjects ability to draw conclusions from the premises presented—massively so in the second experiment. However, in neither experiment was there any evidence that the size of the belief bias effect was increased by the use of more complex problems. This clear—and counter-intuitive result—provides strong support for the Selective Scrutiny model over its rival.

Conclusions

The Selective Scrutiny model of belief bias favoured in this discussion (and that of Barston, 1986) provides an explanation of this phenomenon which is highly compatible with accounts of other biases which I have discussed in previous chapters. The model is clearly in line with the heuristic/analytic theory of Evans (1984a)—a theory devised on the basis of quite different data such as the matching bias effect in the selection task. This theory proposes in general that representational heuristics precede logical analysis and cause the latter to be applied to selective aspects of the problem content. Belief bias is an example of such a heuristic which results in selective lack of logical scrutiny in the case of obviously believable conclusions. Such "short-circuiting" would of course explain the correlation between belief bias and the absence of reference to the premises in the protocols collected by Evans et al. (1983). More generally, it underlines the theme of selective processing resulting in subjects' failure to exhibit underlying competence which I have emphasised throughout this book.

If this view of belief bias is accepted, the question still arises as to why people employ a belief heuristic leading to selective scrutiny of logical arguments. Those favouring the orthodox interpretation of the confirmation bias studies discussed in Chapter Three might well see the two phenomena as closely connected and related to what social psychologists call "belief preservation" (see, for example, Nisbett & Ross, 1980, Chapter Eight). Hence, one way of maintaining beliefs is to attempt to avoid falsifying evidence (confirmation bias) whilst the other involves selective attempts to discredit such evidence once it is encountered. An alternative possibility is that cognitive economy requires that we do not constantly question the basis of knowledge which we hold to be true and that it is quite reasonable to examine evidence only when it is in conflict with our beliefs. Pollard (1982) argues strongly along these lines that belief bias reflects more rational behaviour in real life than the laboratory studies would suggest.

So far, the emphasis has been on the biasing effects of prior knowledge in reasoning. We now consider the hypothesis that knowledge may result in more logical and appropriate reasoning.

DEBIASING EFFECTS OF KNOWLEDGE

As indicated earlier, the notion that the use of realistic content facilitates logical reasoning dates back at least to Wilkins (1928). Belief in this hypothesis was promoted by the discussions of early studies of the Wason selection task in the widely-read and influential book on reasoning published by Wason and Johnson-Laird (1972), whose claims were based upon the evidence available at the time. However, as we shall see, subsequent research has considerably complicated the story of how familiar content does in fact influence reasoning.

Of course, some would argue (e.g., Cohen, 1981) that it is not so much a question of the debiasing effects of realistic content as the biasing effects of abstract content. Such theorists propose that artificial laboratory experiments considerably underestimate people's true logical competence. However, even if the facilitating effect of realistic content was as straightforward as this argument supposes, it would still not be an entirely fair argument. Investigation of arbitrary reasoning problems is justified on both theoretical and practical grounds. For example, if you believe that reasoning is achieved by use of a set of general purpose inference rules then you should expect people to be able to reason with arbitrary problems providing that the logical structure is clearly defined. From the practical viewpoint, it is by no means always the case that all real life reasoning takes place with the benefit of highly familiar content and context. Indeed, *explicit* reasoning in everyday life often involves such problems as checking regulations for entitlement to claim grants, or deciding whether or not an insurance policy covers the risk with which you are concerned. Such tasks are not dissimilar to those of many laboratory reasoning experiments—and equally notorious in the difficulty that they cause!

Most of the modern research into the facilitatory effects of realistic content has involved use of the Wason selection task introduced in Chapter Three. A very large number of papers have been published—and continue to be published—on this topic, investigating a variety of detailed issues. It is beyond the scope of this chapter to provide a full review of this work but I will give a brief history and discuss what I consider to be the major findings of interest (a full review of work published up until about 1982 is given by Griggs, 1983). I will also look at the most interesting and general theoretical explanation to have been proposed of findings on this task, namely that of pragmatic reasoning schemas.

Content Effects in the Wason Selection Task

The support from Wason and Johnson-Laird (1972) for the facilitation by realism hypothesis was based upon the findings of two studies available to them at the time of writing. These studies introduced the contents which I will describe as Towns and Transport and as the Postal Rule respectively (see Table 4.3 for a summary description of these and other contents). The first study to report facilitation was that of Wason and Shapiro (1971) in which subjects were shown cards each of which had the name of a town written on one side and a means of transport on the other. Subjects were told that each card represented a journey that the experimenter had made. They were then told to investigate the truth of the claim "Every time I go to Manchester I travel by train" with reference to four cards showing, on their facing sides, "Manchester", "Leeds", "train" and "car".

By analogy to the usual abstract task findings, subjects might be expected to choose "Manchester" and "train", while the correct choice is "Manchester" and *"car"*. A substantial number of subjects did, in fact, choose the correct combination, a facilitation which was significant compared with a control group receiving an abstract letters and numbers version of the problem. More striking, indeed almost universal facilitation was found in the study by Johnson-Laird, Legrenzi, and Legrenzi (1972). Instead of cards they used envelopes which were lying either with the front side exposed—in which case the stamp could be inspected—or else with the back exposed in which case one could see whether or not the envelopes were sealed. Subjects were told to imagine they were postal workers checking the rule "If the letter is sealed then it has a 50 lire stamp on it". The subjects used were English students who were familiar with a now defunct postal rule at the time which required that higher postage be paid for letters mailed in sealed envelopes. Although Italian stamps were used in the condition quoted, it is important to note that the equivalent of the critical not-q card had a

TABLE 4.3
Problem Contents Used in Studies of the Wason Selection Task

TOWNS AND TRANSPORT (Wason & Shapiro, 1971)
"Every time I go to Manchester I travel by train."

Comments: Early reports of facilitatory effects but several recent failures to replicate.

POSTAL RULE (Johnson-Laird, Legrenzi, & Legrenzi, 1972)
"If the letter is sealed then it has a 50 lire stamp on it."

Comments: Strong facilitation of logical performance, but restricted to population groups familiar with such a rule in real life.

FOOD AND DRINKS (Manktelow & Evans, 1979)
"If I eat haddock then I drink gin."

Comments: No facilitation.

DRINKING AGE RULE (Griggs & Cox, 1982)
"If a person is drinking beer then that person must be over 19 years of age."

Comments: Strong and reliable facilitation.

CLOTHING RULE (Cox and Griggs, 1982)
"If a person is wearing blue then the person must be over 19 years of age."

Comments: Facilitation only if preceded by the drinking age rule.

SEARS PROBLEM (D'Andrade, described by Griggs, 1983)
"If a purchase exceeds $30, then the receipt must be approved by the departmental manager."

Comments: Facilitates, even though subjects have no direct experience of the context.

---

lower value, 40 lire stamp on it (a second not-q card had no stamp at all). Almost all subjects correctly checked sealed envelopes (p) and those not bearing 50 lire stamps.

Neither of these problem contents has worn too well with time. Several replications of the Towns and Transport effects were reported in the early literature, but the effectiveness of this content was later called into question, initially by Manktelow and Evans (1979). They consistently failed to find any facilitation in a series of four experiments using arbitrarily realistic rules concerning relationships between food and drinks taken at the same meal, despite the manipulation of several variables including group versus individual testing. In a final experiment, however, they attempted a straight replication of the Wason and Shapiro study and found equal lack of effect. In the discussion of the paper they also suggested that the facilitation observed by Johnson-Laird et al. might well have been due to the fact that the rule corresponded directly to the real postal rule in subjects' experience. They suggested that subjects might have been retrieving the solution from memory (understamped envelopes must be sealed) rather than reasoning *per se*. This was subsequently described as the "memory cue" hypothesis by Griggs and Cox (1982).

Various authors in the reasoning literature have recently attributed to me the belief that realistic contents only facilitate reasoning by direct cueing of memory. I don't think that I ever believed that and I certainly do not do so now as the following discussion will make clear. This most definitely was not the thrust of Manktelow and Evans' argument, which instead proposed that permitting direct use of memory cues constituted a methodological flaw to be avoided in future research. On the basis of this argument and their own experiments they suggested only that the apparently well-established facilitation by realism effect was not clearly proven and required further investigation. That it has most certainly received!

Griggs and Cox (1982) reported three well-designed and pertinent experiments. The first involved an Americanised version of the Towns and Transport content which produced no facilitation. Following the arguments of Manktelow and Evans, they then presented their subjects with a version of the Postal Rule which produced, as predicted, no facilitation with their American subjects who had had no relevant real life experience with such a rule. An independent study by Yachanin and Tweney (1982) of the same two contents on American student subjects also reported no facilitation. Further confirmation for the memory cue explanation of the Postal Rule problem comes from a study by Golding (1981) who found in a study of British subjects that only the *older* ones showed a significant facilitation effect with this content—presumably because they had had past experience with the real life version of the rule.

Griggs and Cox (1982) also, however, sought to find positive evidence for the memory cue hypothesis by choosing content which would relate to their own subjects' experiences. Their third experiment introduced the Drinking Age rule which produced very substantial facilitation of logically correct choices. The rule "If a person is drinking beer then that person must be over 19 years of age", was based on the actual drinking law in the state of Florida where the experiment was conducted. Their student subjects were very familiar with this rule—and doubtless with the practice of breaking it in a number of cases too. The four cards each represented a person drinking in a bar with the beverage written on one side and their age on the other. Most subjects correctly chose to turn over cards showing "beer" rather than "coke" (p) and also to examine those marked with ages under rather than over 19 (not-q).

Griggs (1983) claims that there is no evidence that logical *reasoning* as opposed to performance is being facilitated by the use of those realistic contents, such as the Drinking Age rule, which reliably affect choices. He does, however, extend the memory cueing hypothesis to include also "reasoning by analogy" in the light of other findings. One reason for this is the transfer effects reported by Cox and Griggs (1982) who found that a structurally similar Clothing Age rule (see Table 4.3) produced significantly improved performance compared with an abstract control, but only if presented *after* a problem using the Drinking Age rule. Another reason is the existence of a facilitatory content known as the Sears Problem (cf. Table 4.3) in which subjects play the role of department store managers clearing sales receipts. The point here is that the subjects do not have directly relevant experience of this role, though they may bring analogous experience to bear. As Griggs mentions, schema theory might be an appropriate means of explaining such analogical reasoning, an approach which will be discussed shortly.

Several recent studies have varied the precise nature of the Drinking Age problem in an attempt to find out precisely what causes the facilitation. For example, Yachanin and Tweney (1982) suggested that the effect might simply result from a difference of wording in the instructions. Whereas the subjects are usually asked to decide whether the "rule is true or false", Griggs and Cox's subjects were asked to decide whether the rule was being *violated*. A series of studies have investigated the effect of this instructional factor on the Drinking Age content, and on abstract and other contents (Griggs, 1984; Chrostowski & Griggs, 1985; Valentine, 1985; Yachanin, 1986). The findings were remarkably clear and consistent across studies. As Griggs (1984) puts it, the "violates" instruction is neither sufficient nor necessary for facilitation, since (a) its introduction into abstract versions of the task is unhelpful and (b) the Drinking Age content facilitates even when the standard "true or false" instruction is used. However, it does appear that the facilitation is greater when the "violates" instruction is used—possibly because it gives subjects the falsification set appropriate to the solution.

Pollard and Evans (1987) introduced other manipulations to investigate the Drinking Age content. They distinguished between the actual content of the rule and the cards, and the context or scenario in which it is placed. Their findings suggest that both an appropriate content and context are required for facilitation. This is most clearly shown in their second experiment in which an edited version of the problem omitting reference to the police officer checking people in a bar was used. In this version they were simply told that a drink was written on one side of the card and a number of years on the other and asked to check whether the cards conformed to the rule: 'If there is beer on a card then the number of years old is over 18'. Despite the necessary modification in wording to the rule (so that it refers explicitly to the cards) the full scenario version was as effective as always, whereas the edited version produced no better performance than the letter/number control version. This version used the rule "If there is a B on one side then there is a number over 18 on the other", together with the cards B, C, 22 and 16. One group were given this rule with the policeman scenario and told tht B and C stood for beer and coke and the numbers for ages, but despite this attempt to introduce an effective "detective set" into the abstract problem, very little facilitation was observed.

Clearly, Griggs and Cox's (1982) original Drinking Age problem was presented in a manner which was maximally effective. It appears from subsequent work that both an appropriate content and context are necessary and the set to investigate violations of the rule augments the effect. It is not enough simply to phrase the problems in everyday content, nor to emphasise falsification in the instructions. A semantically coherent content and context must be created in which the subject can apply the actions that would be appropriate in real life. The kind of memory structure that would appear well able to account for this, along with the evidence of reasoning by analogy, is the schema.

Pragmatic Reasoning Schemas and the Wason Selection Task

The schema approach to reasoning theory was introduced in Chapter One. As a brief reminder, a schema is a knowledge structure which is induced or learned from experience, contains a cluster of related declarative and procedural knowledge, and is sensitive to the domain and context of the current focus of cognitive activity. The pragmatic reasoning schema, as espoused by Cheng and Holyoak (1985) is a structure of intermediate level of abstraction, more abstract than content specific knowledge cueing but more specific than general purpose inference rules. A schema is something which is elicited from memory and fitted to the current problem by virtue of (a) its domain relevance and (b) its structural similarity. Once elicited, a schema includes procedural knowledge in the form of rules or heuristics which can be applied to the problem in hand.

Schema theory would seem to provide a good explanation of the kinds of results on the Wason selection task that have been discussed above. It can explain the general contextual dependency findings, the reasoning by analogy discussed by Griggs (1983), and the importance of combining familiar content with an appropriate scenario and set of instructions. Various authors have discussed the potential relevance of this theoretical concept to selection task findings (for example, Rumelhart, 1980; Griggs, 1983; Wason, 1983). However, the first experimental studies to be specifically designed on this basis are those reported by Cheng and Holyoak (1985).

Cheng & Holyoak identified a common feature of the problem contents shown to be successful in facilitating logical performance on the selection task such as the Postal Rule (for those with relevant real life experience), the Drinking Age rule, and the Sears Problem (see Table 4.3). They suggested that the key to successful reasoning with each of these lies in the retrieval and application by the subjects of a *permission schema*. The variables in this schema are for a "precondition" and an "action", which are related by four production rules embedded within the schema (see Table 4.4). These rules go beyond those of the logic of material implication, for example by including modal terms such as "must" and "may". However, the key point is that the productions of these rules produce card choices which *coincide* with those prescribed by a logical analysis of the selection task.

For example, on the Drinking Age problem the action is drinking alcohol and the precondition is being over 19 years of age. Hence, rule 1 translates as "If alcohol is to be drunk then the person must be over 19 years of age", while rule 4 translates as "If the person is under 19 years of age then they must not drink alcohol". These rules respectively determine checking of people drinking alcohol and those under 19 years of age which is, of course, the correct p and not-q selection. The other two rules result in non-inspection of not-p and q due to the non-imperative terms "need not" and "may".

One of the general findings with work on schema theory in problem solving is that mere possession by the subject of a relevant schema does not suffice. For example, subjects may not use deep structural analogues between one problem and another unless cued to do so by the instructions (Gick & Holyoak, 1983). Hence, the simple use of content to which the permission schema can be applied may not suffice, as in Pollard & Evans' (1987) demonstration that the accompanying policeman scenario is vital. It is less clear why an invitation to role playing alone is sufficient for the Sears Problem but not the Postal Rule, in which real life experience of a similar rule in the same domain appears necessary.

Cheng and Holyoak (1985) presented several selection task experiments in support of their pragmatic reasoning theory. In the first they showed that provision of a rationale for an otherwise arbitrary permission rule was necessary for facilitation unless the subjects could provide it from their own experience—the exception being demonstrated with Hong Kong students on the Postal Rule problem with which they had recent real life experience. In

TABLE 4.4
Production Rules Embedded in the Permission Schema Proposed by Cheng and Holyoak (1985)

Rule 1: If the action is to be taken, then the precondition must be satisfied.
Rule 2: If the action is not to be taken, then the precondition need not be satisfied.
Rule 3: If the precondition is satisfied, then the action may be taken.
Rule 4: If the precondition is not satisfied, then the action must not be taken.

another experiment they attempted to demonstrate the abstract nature of reasoning schemas by using a rule of the actual form, "If one is to take action A, then one must first satisfy precondition P" which produced significant facilitation relative to the usual type of abstract letters and numbers problem. A later study by Cheng, Holyoak, Nisbett, and Olilver (1986) identified a second type of schema, based upon obligations, which maps on to correct performance on the selection task. They found that training subjects specifically on the use of the obligation schema facilitated performance on problems of this type whereas training in general conditional logic did not.

CONTENT EFFECTS IN STATISTICAL REASONING

As indicated earlier in the chapter, research on the effects of content and context on reasoning has been principally confined to studies of deductive reasoning which have been the focus of the preceding sections. Despite the relative neglect of content effects in statistical reasoning research, there are a few recent studies worth mentioning which bear directly on the theoretical issues with which this chapter is concerned.

Evans, Brooks, and Pollard (1985) investigated the role of prior beliefs in statistical reasoning and included an attempt to demonstrate belief bias effects of a type analogous to those found in deductive reasoning studies. They point out that while Bayesian decision theory emphasises the rational role of prior belief, actual studies of the base rate fallacy (see Chapter Two) have generally involved the use of prior probabilities presented as arbitrary statistics. Evans et al. (1985) investigated the possibility that prior probablilities determined by actual beliefs of the subjects would influence statistical judgements in the correct manner. To test for belief bias, they also gave people a statistical question whose answer should be independent of prior beliefs about the problem materials. They found that beliefs significantly influenced subjects' responses to both questions, but significantly more so on the question where it was normatively appropriate. These findings are quite compatible with those of Evans et al. (1983) in which both logic and belief were found to influence reasoning. More generally, they tie in with the mass of evidence discussed by Evans (1982) that the data of most reasoning experiments reflect a combination of logical and non-logical tendencies.

The hypothesis that reasoning may be facilitated by familiarity with content and context has also received some attention in recent studies of statistical reasoning. This work forms part of the same broad research programme as that which includes the work on pragmatic reasoning schemas, discussed in the previous section, and is published within an important series of recent research papers on both statistical and logical reasoning conducted by various subsets of the authors Nisbett, Holyoak, Cheng, Fong, Krantz and other colleagues. These studies, and the resulting theoretical perspective, are summarised by Holland, Holyoak, Nisbett, & Thagard (1986, Chapters

Eight and Nine). The theoretical explanation of content effects in reasoning which they propose is a rather curious hybrid of the inference rule and schema approach. In essence, for statistical reasoning they suggest that people reason by use of general rules of thumb, such as the law of large numbers, with accuracy dependent upon the subjects' knowledge of the characteristics of the domain in question. On the other hand, they accept the general consensus (Rips and Braine excepted) that logical rules do not form the basis of deductive reasoning and argue instead for pragmatic reasoning schemas. This rather strange position appears to have been forced by the conflicting findings of the authors with the two types of inference.

The view of statistical inference taken by Holland et al. appears to rely heavily on the evidence of two studies in particular. The first, by Nisbett, Krantz, Jepson, and Kunda (1983) is one of the few to have looked in detail at content effects in statistical reasoning. One of the main types of inference with which they were concerned was that of generalising from instances. They predicted, and observed, that people's willingness to make generalisations from small samples of evidence would depend upon their knowledge of, or belief about, the variability of the objects concerned. Hence, and in accordance with statistical theory, people were more willing to generalise about characteristics or objects thought to have low variability. What they suggest here is that people have a reasonable statistical rule but that the accuracy of their reasoning depends upon the correctness of their assumptions about the objects. For example, Holland et al. point out that social stereotyping causes people to underestimate the variability of out-groups relative to in-groups with consequential inferential errors. Nisbett et al. (1983) succeeded in altering people's inferences by manipulations which changed their perception of variability. These authors also provided evidence relevant to the "facilitation by realism" hypothesis by relating the explanations from their subjects of statistical events in the domain of sports and acting to their degree of experience in those domains. They found that statistical explanations were given more often by the more knowledgeable subjects.

The other major influence on the discussion of Holland et al. is the work on training statistical inference by Fong, Krantz, and Nisbett (1986) who found that abstract training with statistical principles in the laboratory facilitated reasoning with everyday problems involving probability as did attendance at courses of formal instruction in statistics. The contrast with the findings of Cheng et al. (1986)—who reported neither laboratory nor course-based training in logical reasoning to facilitate performance on the selection task—appears to be crucial in their proposal of the hybrid rules/ schemas reasoning theory. The training studies of these authors will be considered further in Chapter Six. Meanwhile, it is worth noting that their view of statistical inference is reasonably compatible with the review of work on the law of large numbers in Chapter Two of this book, from which it appears that people do have some general, domain independent understanding that larger samples produce more reliable evidence, albeit in the form of a fragile and easily disrupted intuition.

DISCUSSION AND CONCLUSIONS

The main focus of this chapter has been the consideration of the effects of content on deductive inference. We have seen that the theory of pragmatic reasoning schemas seems to provide a good explanation of the work on the Wason selection task. Certainly, people retrieve something from memory that helps them, and the importance of scenario, instructional sets, and the ability to reason by analogy all suggest that this is something more abstract than direct memory of a real life equivalent of the rule. A problem for schema theory, however, pointed out by Johnson-Laird (personal communication), is the logical competence which people manifest on deductive reasoning problems couched in abstract terms. Admittedly, such competence is minimal on the selection task, but most abstract problems in conditional and syllogistic logic show substantial influence of logic on subjects' inferences, albeit in combination with a variety of biases (cf. Evans, 1982).

Johnson-Laird's (1983) mental models theory of reasoning might provide an alternative explanation for the content effects on the selection task. The theory assumes that people reason by constructing alternative models compatible with the information given and by searching for counter-examples. Rather than evoking schemas, it may be that people's knowledge of the facilitatory context helps them to construct appropriate models and find the counter-examples. However, Johnson-Laird's theory faces an equal and opposite problem to that which he poses for schema theory, namely that of explaining why reasoning performance on the abstract selection task is so extremely poor. It would seem from his general description of the theory that such a task would be quite straightforward. Firstly, the modelling requires only the projection of alternative values onto the backs of cards one at a time—no great strain on working memory. Secondly, we know from other research on conditional reasoning that subjects should have little difficulty in recognising the counter-example of a true antecedent and false consequent. So why don't people solve the problem?

My own view (cf. Evans, 1984a)—which in a sense lets everyone off—is that there is precious little evidence that the Wason selection task induces *any* form of reasoning, certainly not in its abstract form. The point is that the instruction to investigate cards appears to result in purely *heuristic* assessment of the cards based on their exposed sides. In a sense the instructions virtually require subjects to make a relevance judgement which I suggest will precede any form of analytic reasoning. This, of course, explains the matching bias effects as discussed in Chapter Three. Even with realistic materials, it is not clear that subjects actually apply inferential rules (schema theory) or analyse possible models of hidden values (mental models theory). All that actually is required is for the subjects to retrieve sufficient knowledge from memory to determine that the perceived relevance of the exposed cards corresponds to the logical solution. The fact that context and scenario are needed as well as content (Cheng & Holyoak, 1985; Pollard & Evans, 1987) might simply be because these determine that "potential violator" is the criterion for relevance and provide cues that the not-q card falls into this category.

I do, however, regard the selection task as quite exceptional in this regard and believe that most deductive reasoning problems, such as classical syllogisms, induce a mixture of reasoning and bias. In the case of the belief bias effect, the discussion given earlier favoured the Selective Scrutiny model (Fig. 4.1) in which it is assumed that reasoning may be by-passed by heuristic evaluation based on the believability of the conclusion. However, a reasoning stage is clearly also assumed to explain the strong effects of logic on the inferences observed. The model discussed earlier made no assumptions about the nature of the mechanism used when subjects attempt to decide whether the conclusion is determined by the premises. It seems unlikely that people would possess inference rules applicable to classical syllogisms, and pragmatic reasoning schemas do not seem relevant here. I personally feel the mental models theory put forward by Johnson-Laird and Bara (1984) to be the most convincing explanation in the literature of how people may draw appropriate inferences from quantified premises. However, I do not believe there is necessarily a singular method of reasoning to be applied to all problems, and it must be said that the mental models theory has so far received very little testing outside of the domain of syllogistic inference.

The central point arising from the discussion of belief bias—in this book orientated towards the explanation of biases rather than reasoning mechanisms—is that knowledge can induce biases by *pre-empting* analytic reasoning by whatever means. The other side of the coin—the debiasing effects of knowledge—is also relevant since it may appear to limit the damage when considering expert reasoning. There is, however, uncertainty at present as to whether beneficial effects of knowledge occur through enhanced representation of the relevant features of the problem or because of the importation of new procedural knowledge in the form of domain sensitive rules and heuristics. Perhaps both.

5 Self-knowledge

The study of self-knowledge, or *metacognition* as it is sometimes known, is concerned with the question of how much people know about their own knowledge. This question in various forms has attracted the attention of psychologists interested in a variety of topics including perception, memory, developmental and social psychology as well as in the psychology of thinking and reasoning. The reader may, however, be surprised that a whole chapter should be devoted to this topic in a book concerned with biases in reasoning.

In fact, the issue of self-knowledge in thinking and reasoning is of great importance for both theoretical and practical reasons. Firstly, it is central to the theoretical argument of this book that many biases are caused by *preattentive* or *preconscious* heuristic processes which determine selective encoding of psychologically "relevant" features of the problem. If this argument is correct it follows that people should be largely unaware of at least one crucial part of their own thought processes and consequently the cause of their bias. Here my theory departs from some other explanations of bias which suggest, even if they do not make it explicit, that errors result from the application of conscious heuristics or strategies. This, for example, is a critical difference between the positivity bias explanation of confirmation bias proposed in Chapter Three and the "positive test strategy" suggested by Klayman and Ha (1987).

One practical implication of the proposal that biases result from unconscious processes is for approaches to *debiasing*, the topic to be addressed in Chapter Six. For example, a bias resulting from an explicitly held and consciously applied strategy might be expected to be correctable by verbal instruction, whereas one resulting from a preconscious heuristic might require a different approach. It is also by no means self-evident that the procedural knowledge underlying what Evans (1984a) calls the analytic processes responsible for subsequent reasoning is consciously accessible either. If such procedural knowledge is frequently implicit also, then further methodological and practical implications arise concerning the problem of knowledge acquisition or elicitation. That is to say, introspective reports collected by psychologists, or interview data collected by knowledge engineers (cf. Evans, 1988) would be at best incomplete and at worst positively misleading.

There are, in fact, two related but distinct propositions about defective self-knowledge. The first is simply that a number of significant cognitive processes are not accessible to consciousness or at least not in a form which can be verbalised. A useful terminological distinction here is between *explicit* cognitive processes which are conscious and verbalisable and *implicit* ones which are not. The second type of defective self-knowledge occurs when people hold inaccurate or false beliefs about their thought processes. For example, they may overestimate what they know, or believe that a certain type of stimulus or strategy determined their behaviour when in fact this was not the case. This type of problem has particularly serious consequences for any researcher using self-report methods to investigate someone's knowledge or thought processes. Not only may people be unaware of the process underlying their behaviour but they may also provide a false report upon it.

This chapter provides selective coverage and discussion of the investigation of the problem of self-knowledge in psychology. I have selected studies for their relevance to the topic of reasoning, for example by concentrating on metacognition in thinking rather than in memory. If my selection is biased, then it is unconsciously so (!). In the empirical section of the chapter, I discuss evidence relating to the two propositions identified above, i.e. lack of awareness and false self-beliefs. In the theoretical section, however, I shall consider some of the recent debate and controversy concerning this subject, especially with regard to the interpretation of verbal reports.

EMPIRICAL STUDIES OF SELF-KNOWLEDGE

Before considering experimental evidence, we should note some *a priori* arguments for the view that many cognitive processes are unconscious or implicit. First it is clear that conscious attention is selective and that pre-attentive processes, i.e. those which determine what we attend to, must themselves be unconscious (or preconscious) or we would have an infinite regress. Hence, when the mention of our name in an unattended conversation at a party causes us to switch attention from the person to whom we were previously listening, this must be caused by an unconscious process. An extension of this argument lies in the more controversial proposal that we are not aware of the nature of any perceptual or cognitive process but only in the *product* which it places in consciousness. For example, consider the phenomenon of size constancy by which the apparent size of distant objects is phenomenally enlarged to compensate for their distance. We cannot discover this phenomenon by introspection because we are aware only of the product—how big things look—and not of the underlying process.

It also takes only a little reflection to realise that we perform many complex cognitive acts without having any idea of how we accomplish them. Hence, we can instantly decide whether a face shown to us in a picture identifies one of the hundreds of individuals we know as opposed to the millions we do not. Would anyone claim to be able to introspect upon the process responsible? Similarly, we all have a massive and highly complex system of implicit procedural knowledge called language by which we can generate and understand a potentially infinite number of grammatical sentences. How many of us could write down even a few of the grammatical rules which this linguistic competence implies?

I contend that the above examples of implicit knowledge are uncontroversial simply because people have no feeling that they possess this knowledge verbally when questioned, though it is undeniable that they in some sense have it. Other proposals of unconscious processing are highly controversial in psychology, however. One of these is the topic of subliminal perception which has been discussed in terms of both the evidence and the surrounding controversy in two books by Dixon (1971; 1981). The controversy is perhaps rather surprising in view of the undeniable fact that unattended (though potentially perceptible) stimuli must influence our behaviour through pre-attentive processes, as proposed previously.

More relevant to this book is the controversy surrounding the proposition that "higher" cognitive processes such as those involved in problem solving, decision making, or social judgement are also inaccessible to conscious inspection (see the discussion of theoretical issues in the latter part of this chapter). Here it appears that the personal conviction of people (in general) that they are aware of the strategies by which they reason, solve problems, and make decisions may cause some other people (a subset of psychologists) to frame their academic theories accordingly. This is why it is important to examine the evidence for false self-belief as well as for lack of awareness as will be done here.

There are many demonstrations in the psychological literature of poor correspondence between task performance and associated verbalisations or introspections (see for example, the reviews of Nisbett & Wilson, 1977, and Dixon, 1981). However, I have chosen three areas of experimental evidence for discussion here which I feel to be of particular relevance to research on reasoning and judgement. The first concerns evidence of implicit learning of complex rules which is indirectly relevant to reasoning and directly relevant to some of the broader theoretical issues to be discussed later in the chapter.

The second involves evidence of false self-knowledge as expressed through subjective judgements of confidence and feeling of knowing. The final topic is that of introspective reports of deductive reasoning processes which I shall argue are not simply incomplete but positively misleading.

Explicit and Implicit Processes in Rule Learning

A number of recent studies have shown that people may acquire and utilise complex rules without any ability to provide evidence of this knowledge through verbalisation. For example, Lewicki, Hill, and Bizot (1988) claim on the basis of their earlier studies (see Lewicki, 1986) that "subjects are able to acquire specific working knowledge (i.e. processing algorithms) not only without being able to articulate what they have learned, but even without being aware that they had learned anything". In the new study reported they used members of their own faculty as subjects to ensure that they were (a) sufficiently articulate to be able to express the nature of the rules and (b) motivated (as psychologists) to try to discover the nature of the experiment. Subjects were required to press one of four keys according to the position on a VDU of a target letter. The positions were in fact determined by a complex but repeated pattern which was shown empirically to have been learned eventually by the subjects (changing the pattern disrupted performance). None, however, came close to identifying the presence of such a pattern in the post-experimental interview.

A set of studies by Reber and colleagues on the learning of rule-based letter strings also provides evidence of implicit processes. The letter strings used were actually productions of artificial finite state grammars which have rules about the permitted transition of one state to another with associated productions of letters. Reber (1976, replicated by Brooks, 1978) showed that learning performance of subjects told explicitly to "discover rules for letter order" was inferior to that of subjects told simply to try to "memorise the letter strings". Subjects in the explicit learning group formulated a number of inaccurate rules unrelated to the underlying grammar. Reber, Kassin, Lewis, and Cantor (1980) argue on the basis of such evidence that "complex structures, such as those underlying language, socialization, perception, and sophisticated games are acquired implicitly and unconsciously".

Work by Donald Broadbent and colleagues on control tasks provides further evidence for the separate nature of explicit and implicit processes. Berry and Broadbent (1984) used a computerised control task set in two separate scenarios—one involved control of the output of the production in a sugar factory and the other an attempt to shift the behaviour of an individual through a simulated social interaction. Each task involved a similar underlying rule relating the value of an independent variable (e.g., size of

work force) to the previous value of the dependent variable (e.g., sugar production) in order to determine the next value of the latter. Subjects were
asked to manipulate the independent variable over a series of trials to
achieve a target level of performance on the dependent variable. In the first
experiment reported, subjects were generally successful in achieving the
target consistently following extensive practice. However, they showed very
little or no ability to demonstrate the knowledge gained when posed direct
questions in a post-experimental questionnaire. Berry and Broadbent make
a similar inference of implicit learning to that proposed by Reber. A second
experiment showed that training by verbal instruction enhanced questionnaire performance but not control task performance, providing strong evidence that separate explicit and implicit processes are involved in the two
types of measure.

In a third experiment, Berry and Broadbent (1984) did find a facilitation
of control performance by verbal instruction but only when it was combined
with a second instruction to "think aloud" while performing the task (the
second manipulation also had no effect on its own). One interpretation of
this finding is that the concurrent verbalisation invoked explicit processing
in the control task itself. A related finding was reported by Berry and Broadbent (1987) on a hypothesis testing task which subjects generally perform
poorly and do not seem able to learn implicitly. They found that a prior
written explanation of the appropriate strategy in combination with concurrent verbalisation facilitated performance, whereas neither manipulation on its own was effective. They comment that: "It seems that where subjects have access to relevant verbal information, concurrent verbalisation
can help maintain attention on the necessary critical aspects".

Broadbent, Fitzgerald, and Broadbent (1986) have reported experiments
on further control tasks involving simulations of transportation and economic systems. In the introduction to this paper, the authors argue strongly
that their work advances upon the many studies in the literature showing a
dissociation between performance and verbalisation in cognitive tasks. They
aim to show that experimental manipulations can affect the probabilities of
successful actions and successful verbalisations independently, hence providing evidence of separate implicit and explicit processes and not simply differing incomplete forms of access to a common database of knowledge.
They demonstrate in their experiments that subjects can have good explicit
knowledge combined with poor implicit knowledge as well as the opposite
combination shown by Berry and Broadbent (1984). This corresponds to the
common real world observation that theoretical knowledge demonstrated in
examinations does not automatically translate into practical application
without extensive experience and training in the real world domain.

Finally, while there is clear evidence that complex rules and strategies
may be learned in an implicit manner it does not seem that this is always so,

and may well be a task dependent result. As mentioned above the task studied by Berry and Broadbent (1987) appears to require the application of explicit knowledge for correct performance. Also relevant is a recent study by Mathews, Buss, Chinn, and Stanley (1988) using a rule learning task where the rule was difficult to discover but easy to state verbally once learned. Using an ingenious split regression technique these authors were able to analyse the sequence of errors across trials into three stages: an initial phase (no learning); a transition phase; and a learned phase. Regular verbal prompts were classified in analogous manner as to the point at which subjects began to show insight into the rule and that where they understood it fully. Throughout several experiments extremely high correlations were observed between the verbal and performance transition points. Moreover, content analysis of the verbalisations provided evidence of correlation between the adoption of good hypothesis testing strategies and speed of learning of the rule. They also failed to dissociate verbal and performance data by introducing experimental manipulations of the kind used by Reber and colleagues. This study points to the need for careful examination of the nature of the tasks used to study explicit and implicit processes and indicates the danger of premature generalisation.

The work discussed in this section, while not involving tasks normally described as "reasoning" problems, is nevertheless directly relevant. For example, control performance requires prediction, and forecasting is a form of inference. Hence, setting a variable according to a rule involves a deductive inference of the consequence for comparison with the target. The results of the studies suggest that: (1) complex rule systems are often, though not always, acquired and applied in an implicit manner; and that (2) explicit, verbalisable processes are distinct from implicit ones and susceptible to different variables. This work supports both propositions of poor self-knowledge outlined above. That is to say verbalisations may quite often be both incomplete and misleading.

Confidence in Judgement

One of the best established literatures on metacognition concerns subjective confidence in intuitive judgement. The term "intuitive", in the context of such research, is generally used to refer to judgements made without the benefit of formal theories or instruments such as computer models. In other words they are judgements made on the basis of what people "feel" to be appropriate. However, a little reflection will confirm that such informal intuitive judgements nevertheless play a large part in the decision making of doctors, managers, scientists, and indeed experts and ordinary people of all kinds.

One form of such intuitive judgement concerns forecasting of future events. Most decisions we make are risky in the sense that they involve uncertainty concerning the outcomes that will result from our choices. Normative decision theory prescribes that we should estimate the probability of alternative outcomes and weigh these against the associated costs and benefits. However, it is far from clear how we can learn to make such probabilistic judgements accurately. Most decisions involve one-off events and it is in the nature of probabilistic events that anything can happen. For example, if I argue with a friend about the result of a football match, expressing 90% confidence about the chances of one side to which he gives only a 20% chance, how will we ever know who was right? One side or the other will win, but nature will not provide any clear feedback on the true probability.

The perhaps artificial solution to this problem which has been adopted by experimental psychologists is to ask people to make judgements about many similar items, each with associated degrees of confidence, and then make statistical comparisons over the whole data set (often averaging over subjects as well). The most popular paradigm involves presenting subjects with general knowledge questions to which two alternative answers are given, one of which is always correct. Subjects must make a forced choice and then provide a probability between 0.5 and 1 which effectively forecasts the likelihood that they are right. Suppose you take all the items for which subjects gave a given rating, say 0.7, and then check on how many occasions such items were actually correctly answered. A perfectly "calibrated" subject would have around 70% of such items correct.

Lichtenstein, Fischhoff, and Phillips (1982) review the large number of such studies which had been conducted up until 1980. Many of these studies plot calibration curves between the objective and subjective accuracy probabilities associated with items. There are two characteristic findings: (1) subjective and objective probabilities are correlated, i.e. if you think that you are more likely to be right then you probably are; and (2) subjective probabilties consistently exceed objective probabilities, hence if you think you have an 80% chance of being right you may in reality have only a 70% chance. This latter finding means that people consistently overestimate what they know and is generally regarded as *overconfidence*—a clear bias of metacognition.

How worried should we be about this overconfidence finding? Perhaps it is specific to the nature of the task, or perhaps simply to do with people's difficulty in expressing confidence judgements as numerical probability estimates. Perhaps it is a problem for laboratory subjects and not for experts in a real world domain. As we shall see, research does not provide much reason for comfort on any of these grounds. For example, people can surely understand what it means to predict with *certainty*, i.e. to give a probability of 1 or 0 to indicate that an event will always or never happen. Yet Fischhoff, Slovic, and Lichtenstein (1977) found that people made substantial use of such extreme predictions, resulting in gross overconfidence—subjective "never" and "always" corresponding to about 20% and 80% objective probabilities respectively.

What about expertise? Well, a ray of hope is given by several studies of American weather forecasters (described by Lichtenstein et al., 1982) who have issued precipitation probability forecasts since 1965. They show near perfect calibration, i.e. it rains or snows on 60% of the days for which they gave 60% precipitation forecasts. However, weather forecasters enjoy advantages which are rare if not unique among professional judges. First, they have well established meteorological theories and good data on which to base their judgements. Second, they make frequent judgements under comparable circumstances. Finally, they get speedy and unambiguous feedback on the correctness of their decisions. Typically, none of these conditions will obtain for most professional makers of risky decisions, for example a manager deciding whether or not to risk the development and marketing of a new product. Most other studies of expert judges reviewed by Lichtenstein et al. do, in fact, show poor calibration and overconfidence comparable to the laboratory studies of student populations.

One paper in this literature is of particular theoretical relevance to issues discussed in this book. Koriat, Lichtenstein, and Fischhoff (1980) attempted to debias confidence judgements by asking subjects to write down reasons for and against the question set before making their decision—yes/no with associated confidence probability. This manipulation did significantly improve calibration and reduce overconfidence relative to a control group and interesting findings also resulted from analysing the nature of the reasons given. In the discussion of the paper the authors suggest that the task has two cognitive stages, the first involving searching of one's knowledge and the second reviewing evidence and assessing confidence. They also attach a proposed bias to each stage—the first in favour of positive rather than negative information, because subjects seek more evidence for than against the question. The second bias is to disregard evidence inconsistent with the chosen answer. These two biases have a clear correspondence with the positivity bias and belief bias effects discussed in earlier chapters of this book in explanation of performance on quite different kinds of reasoning tasks.

Overconfidence effects are not limited to the paradigm employed in the calibration studies. A related phenomenon has, for example, been shown in a different set of studies on probability judgement, a number of which are reviewed by Fischhoff (1982). In these studies subjects are asked to assess the *a priori* probabilities of events with or without knowledge of what the outcome actually was. The general finding is that subjects' estimates are influenced by the presence of outcome knowledge. If they are told that a particular outcome did, in fact, occur then they rate its prior probability higher than do subjects not told the outcome. Similarly, knowledge that an event did not occur lowers estimates of its prior likelihood. In other words people habitually overestimate what they could have predicted in advance—a phenomenon known as hindsight bias or the knew-it-all-along-effect. This is, of course, another error of metacognition comparable to overconfidence—people have a self-flattering idea of their own knowledge.

The first demonstration of hindsight bias in the judgement literature appears to be that of Fischhoff (1975) although there have been a number of replications (see Fischhoff, 1982). In his 1975 paper, Fischhoff presented subjects with passages of text providing descriptions of historical events, for example of a battle between British and Gurkha forces in India. Subjects were asked to assess the likelihood of a number of different outcomes—in the above example, of a British victory, a Gurkha victory or of a military stalemate with or without a peace settlement. In addition they were asked to rate the relevance to the outcome of each different piece of information presented in the text. One (control) group made their judgements without outcome knowledge while four others were told that one or another of the four alternatives was the "true" one.

Hindsight bias was demonstrated by highly consistent and significant increases in likelihood rating of the given outcome relative to the control group. Of particular interest, however, were the relevance ratings which also proved to be highly dependent upon outcome knowledge. Essentially, subjects judged items favouring the stated outcome to be more relevant. These findings appear to relate to the distinctions between implicit and explicit processes, and between performance and explanations dealt with elsewhere in this chapter. It appears that judgements are unconsciously biased by outcome knowledge and then subsequently justified by a selective reference to supportive evidence. There is a close similarity here to the claim of Wason and Evans (1975), to be discussed shortly, that verbal reports of reasoning strategies may be *rationalisations* of unconsiously determined biases.

Finally, some recent work on metacognition in problem solving is of relevance here. Metcalfe and Wiebe (1987) demonstrated that "feeling of knowing", i.e. belief that a problem had been solved, was uncorrelated with actual success on tasks traditionally regarded as "insight problems", and that "feeling of warmth" ratings were unpredictive of progress on the same type of problem. Both metacognitions proved to have some validity, however, when applied to algebra problems in which success is achieved through a series of clear substages—a further demonstration of the task dependency of experimental results. On both types of problem subjects showed substantial overconfidence when asked to predict the proportion of problems which they had correctly solved.

The studies discussed in this section provide further cause for serious doubt about the accuracy of people's metacognitions. Not only may the causes of inferences and judgements be implicit or unconscious, but explicit assessments of self-knowledge may be optimistic and misleading. The same theme is developed with more specific reference to introspective verbal reports in the next section.

Verbal Reports of Reasoning Strategies

Some readers may object that most of the evidence so far presented for implicit cognitive processes relates to relatively low-level tasks. Control strategies may be complex, but so is driving a car and most would accept that such skilled activity is carried out at a largely unconscious or "automatic" level—at least once it is highly practised. Judgement based on subjective intuitions and feelings might again be thought a special case. Surely, a verbal reasoning task must induce an explicit sequence of mental processes of which the reasoner is aware and able to articulate?

In looking at this question, it is important to recognise that rather different issues arise according to the difficulty level of the problems and the observed competence of the reasoning. Consider first the case where subjects are predominantly competent. An example is provided by transitive reasoning problems of the sort, "Jane is taller than Mary, Sarah is shorter than Mary, who is tallest?" Subjects make few errors on such problems and the main dependent variable of interest has been response latency (see Evans, 1982, Chapter Four for a review). Clearly, then, subjects are reasoning on this task, so we might expect them to be able to provide verbal reports of their strategies, assuming that an explicit cognitive process is involved.

In fact, the history of research on transitive inferences suggests, if anything, that experimenters have been misled by their subjects' introspections. One of the main theories is that subjects construct a mental representation of the three terms in the form of a visual image whose spatial properties determines the relative ease of problem solution. The founders of this theory were much influenced by the introspective accounts of strategies offered by their subjects (cf. de Soto, London, & Handel, 1965; Huttenlocher, 1968) as have been some subsequent researchers (e.g., Quinton & Fellows, 1975). However, the success of the imagery theory in predicting problem difficulty is based purely upon its structural assumptions about information processing and the data are fitted equally well by a model based upon entirely different, linguistic principles (Clark, 1969). In fact, Sternberg (1980) has provided evidence that a model combining features of both imagery and linguistic models fits the data better than either original theory.

The question is how do we know whether subjects are "using imagery"—whatever that might mean—other than by the fact that their introspections suggest it? The best approach is to seek converging evidence by relating reasoning performance to such variables as the spatial abilities of the subjects, the modality of the problem presentation or the concreteness of the problem materials. Although success for such an approach was claimed by Shaver, Pierson, and Lang (1975), this study contained several methodological flaws which I have identified previously (see Evans, 1982, pp 61–62). More carefully controlled studies reported subsequently have failed to find any objective evidence that visual cognition is involved in transitive inference (see Newstead, Manktelow, & Evans, 1982; Richardson, 1987). Richardson (1987) has made so bold as to state that "The appropriate conclusion seems to be that mental imagery plays no role at all in transitive inference".

Whilst I agree with Richardson, I know that many psychologists would be reluctant so to fly in the face of subjects' introspective reports. The problem lies in the attitude which different authors hold to mental experience and the relationship it has with cognitive processes. In part at least it is a methodological problem. You can have an experimental psychology of cognition or a phenomenological study of consciousness. If the two produce conflicting answers then people fall back on their basic faith in the method and purpose of the subject. To return to my central theme, however, the lesson from the transitive reasoning literature is that even when a deductive reasoning task is involved and successful reasoning is observed, the verbal accounts produced by subjects can be unhelpful or misleading. They certainly are not to be trusted as evidence about cognitive processes in the absence of more objective evidence.

When we consider reasoning tasks which are subject to frequent error or bias, the role of verbal reports becomes even more questionable. One of the most error prone tasks, of course, is the Wason selection task presented with artificial problem content. I have argued in previous chapters that the predominant error on this task, "matching bias", reflects the operation of an unconscious heuristic process which encodes matching cards as relevant and directs attention selectively towards them. If this is indeed the case, how might we expect subjects' verbally reported strategies to look? Clearly we would not expect them to recognise that they are merely matching, especially in view of the instructions to attempt to check the truth or falsity of the rule. It is to be expected from the Berry and Broadbent studies that verbal instructions will impact on the subjects' verbalisations and explanations, if not on their overall task performance.

Subjects' verbalisations about their reasoning were actually studied on the Wason selection task from the earliest work on this problem, before the discussion of content effects became the main issue. Several of these involved attempts at "therapy" based upon confronting the subjects with the contradictions resulting from their own reasoning, for example by showing them that the not-q card—which they declined to select—has a p on the back

(Wason, 1969; Wason & Johnson-Laird, 1970; Wason & Golding, 1974). The characteristic finding of these studies was that subjects showed verbal recognition of the logical consequences of their choices but were very reluctant to change their actual selections as a consequence. Wason and his colleagues were struck by the inconsistencies and self-contradictions in their subjects' protocols and also by the apparent independence of the processes responsible for card selections and those underlying the verbal evaluations enforced by the therapy manipulations.

In spite of this, Goodwin and Wason (1972) offered retrospective verbal explanations collected from their subjects as evidence for the degree of insight underlying their card choices. Specifically, these reports appeared to show the degree of insight into the need for falsification as opposed to verification which was predicted by the model of Johnson-Laird and Wason (1970a). Subjects' explanations correlated sensibly with their behaviour: those choosing not-q were much more likely to indicate that they were attempting to falsify the rule.

Doubt was cast upon the true nature of the insight shown by Goodwin and Wason's subjects with the first report of matching bias by Evans and Lynch (1973). It will be recalled that matching behaviour can look like either verification or falsification according to where the negative component is placed in the rule—the innovation in the method of Evans and Lynch. Hence, Wason and Evans (1975) tested subjects with rules of the form "If p then not q" as well as "If p then q" with half receiving the negative rule prior to the affirmative and half the other way around. Verbal justifications for each card choice were collected as in the Goodwin and Wason study. What happened was that subjects' choices largely followed matching bias so that they tended to choose p and q on both rules. The verbal justifications, however, varied markedly between the two types of rule.

On the negative rule—where matching resulted in logically correct choices—the justifications were in terms of falsification. For example, the subject might say she was turning the p card because a q on the back could disprove the rule. However, the same subject if given the affirmative rule subsequently was prone to give the sort of protocol which Goodwin and Wason had classified as showing "no insight". That is she might say that p was turned to check for a q on the back and vice versa. Subjects are clearly thinking *about* the matching cards—both on the facing and hidden sides—when giving these explanations. Also their explanations respect the logic of the task, so that they only refer to falsification when this would in fact be the consequence of the choice. However, it is hard to believe that a true insight was being induced by the presence of a negative and equally dramatically removed by its absence.

Wason & Evans put forward a dual process theory of reasoning which will be discussed in the next section. The specific interpretation offered of their findings was, however, that card selections were caused by an unconscious matching bias while the verbal explanations were essentially *rationalisations*. In support of this argument, Evans and Wason (1976) presented the selection task to subjects together with a "solution" and asked them to justify it. In fact the correct solution plus three common wrong solutions were given to subjects in four different groups. The majority of subjects provided explanations of whatever solution they happened to get and expressed high confidence that their explanation was correct. No subject indicated any doubt that the solution supplied was correct.

These findings have not deterred some subsequent authors from analysing verbal justifications on the selection task, recording some, though not in my view sufficient caution in the light of the Wason and Evans papers. A typical example is that of Hoch and Tschirgi (1985) who comment that, "Although retrospective protocols may contain elements of rationalisation...and may not always reflect the psychological processes underlying performance, they can supplement the more objective data". This supplementation argument for introspective data is also made by some imagery researchers (e.g., Kosslyn, 1980) and I must admit that I fail to understand it in either context. Hoch and Tschirgi, for example, are impressed by the logical consistency of subjects' explanations of card choices (also observed by Wason and Evans) and quite clearly interpret the explanations as inferences drawn while subjects were solving the task and not as possible *post hoc* justifications. The relationship between the explanations and educational ability levels that they report may only be demonstrating that the more educated have a more articulate facility for rationalisation!

But what of the Evans, Barston, and Pollard (1983) study, discussed at length in Chapter Four. Did we not also employ verbal protocol analysis? Yes, but with the following crucial differences: (1) concurrent verbalisation protocols were used in addition to retrospective ones, and the major analyses based upon this method (concurrent protocols are much less prone to rationalisation for reasons to be discussed later in the chapter); (2) suitable caution was shown about making any causal inferences concerning the correlations observed between protocol content and reasoning behaviour; and (3) the analyses were based upon scoring of what was mentioned by the subject and in what order. In other words the protocols were used as sources of information about the locus of subjects' attention and not as self-reports of mental processes.

This concludes my selective survey of empirical evidence for defective self-knowledge in reasoning. We have seen from three different literatures evidence that processes involved in high-level cognitive performance may be implicit and inaccessible to verbal report. We have also seen that subjects may hold and express false beliefs about their cognitive processes and are liable to mislead the unwary researcher as well, presumably, as themselves. It should also be apparent that these findings raise some important theoretical questions about the nature of human thinking which will now be discussed.

THEORETICAL ISSUES

Wason and Evans (1975) put forward a dual process theory of reasoning to account for the results of their experiment, described above. They put forward the following two fundamental propositions: (1) The processes underlying the reasoning performance, e.g. matching bias, are not generally available to introspective report; and (2) Introspective accounts of performance reflect a tendency for the subjects to *construct* a justification for their own behaviour consistent with their knowledge of the situation. Wason and Evans actually proposed that two distinct forms of thought process underlay selections and justifications which they called Type 1 and Type 2 processes respectively. There is a clear parallel here to the distinction between implicit and explicit processes used by Broadbent and his colleagues. As broader evidence for dual processes, Wason and Evans cited the "therapy" studies on the selection task discussed above in which selection and verbal evaluation processes appeared to be autonomous. They also noted a connection with the findings of Wason (1960) on the 2 4 6 problem, that subjects would perseverate with a confirmed rule but provide alternative verbal formulations of it (see Table 3.1 and the accompanying discussion in Chapter Three).

As a co-author of the dual process theory, I have reformulated the theory in terms of its broader implications more than once (most especially in Evans, 1982, Chapter 12, and in Evans, 1984a). Rather than inflict the history of my personal thinking on the reader, I will present my current views at the end of this chapter with an attempt to provide a coherent explanation of relevant experimental work discussed in this and previous chapters of the book. First, however, it is necessary to discuss the impact of some recent theoretical papers of relevance to this topic, most especially those by Nisbett and Wilson (1977) and Ericsson and Simon (1980).

Nisbett and Wilson (1977) presented a bold and—as it turned out—highly controversial attack on introspection in the context of research on social judgement. In essence, they argued on the same two aspects of defective metacognition that have been referred to throughout this chapter, that is: (1) that people lack awareness of the processes determining their behaviour; and (2) that verbal reports are often inaccurate and misleading. Evidence for lack of awareness was largely based upon people's inability to report the influences shown to have causally affected their behaviour. They cited various experiments on attitude change, for example, in which subjects' reports revealed no awareness of the stimuli influencing them, or even of the fact that a change had occurred at all.

The argument that subjects lack access to mental processes has come under particular attack by a number of subsequent authors. White (1988) in an extensive review of papers stimulated by Nisbett and Wilson has suggested two main lines of criticism: (1) that the distinction between mental processes and their products, which is central to Nisbett and Wilson's argument, is unclear and ill-defined; and (2) that the simple equation of awareness with verbal reportability on which much of their argument rests is unsound. White (1988) in his Table 1 lists 10 possible causes of inaccuracy in a retrospective causal report *other* than lack of access to the process! One such cause, developed in the work of Ericsson and Simon, discussed below, is that the relevant information may have been lost from memory before the report is taken.

White argues that the Nisbett and Wilson proposal should be modified to an argument that verbal reports are inaccurate or incomplete without need to refer to consciousness or awareness. He claims that several experimental studies have falsified this modified hypothesis and also suggests that causal reports, with which Nisbett and Wilson's studies were so concerned, may be exceptionally incomplete compared with other types of verbal report. In spite of these types of criticism it seems to me that much of the evidence for the two types of problems with metacognition still stand from their original paper and indeed are not generally disputed. One is that key stimuli which influence behaviour frequently do go unreported and the second is that reports offered by subjects are often not what they seem to be. Specifically, Nisbett and Wilson suggest that subjects asked to give retrospective reports on their behaviour often do so by constructing causal theories—often based on prior, cultural grounds.

Hence, I believe that the twin arguments of Wason and Evans that reports may omit reference to true causes and provide misleading *post hoc* rationalisations are directly substantiated in the Nisbett and Wilson review of work in social judgement. Where perhaps they (and we) went wrong was in too easily equating such terms as "consciousness" and "awareness" with verbalisation and also in trying to maintain that *all* mental processes are inaccessible to verbal reports. Neither of these contentious assumptions is actually necessary to support the argument of this chapter about the limitations of self-knowledge. The (undisputed) fact that verbal reports are *sometimes* incomplete and *sometimes* misleading is quite serious enough unless one has some way of knowing in advance when a report will be accurate.

Herein lies a point of critical difference in motivation between various authors. My own concern is that we should not be misled by the common sense assumption that reasoning is an introspectible activity so that, for example, we formulate inaccurate reasoning theories on the basis of what our subjects tell us. A critic of my earlier writings on this topic, Morris (1981), appeared more concerned with the philosophical rather than practical implications (as also is White, 1988) in that he argued that because some reports may be rationalisations, or self-hypotheses as he called them, it does not follow that others might not be true strategy reports. My response (Evans, 1981) was that this distinction was of no practical use in the absence of *a priori* criteria for knowing when a report would be one or the other.

The best attempt to provide such *a priori* criteria is that of Ericsson and Simon (1980; 1984). They argued that verbalisations are one of the main forms of data available to cognitive psychologists and that it would be madness to abandon all use of such data because of the difficulties associated with introspective report. Their arguments do not really conflict with those of Wason and Evans or Nisbett and Wilson except in that they wish to emphasise a more positive aspect of verbal reports. The key point is that they regard verbal reports as *data*, i.e. as products which are informative about the processes responsible for them. They do not argue for the traditional introspective approach adopted by authors such as Morris in which reports are regarded as *descriptions* of internal mental processes.

Ericsson and Simon (1984) make it clear very early in their book that they are *not* advocating verbal reports as a valid source of metacognition or self-knowledge. Hence, they say, "It is sometimes believed that using verbal data implies accepting the subjects' interpretation of them or of the events that are reported...However, the issue of the reliability of self-reports can (and, we believe, should) be avoided entirely." The motivation of these authors is to support the validity of verbal protocol analysis of the kind used widely by Newell and Simon (1972) in their classic studies of problem solving. This differs from introspective methods in two crucial respects: (1) verbalisations are collected concurrently rather than retrospectively by instructions to "think aloud" while performing a task; and (2) the protocols are analysed and interpreted by the experimenter, not the subject.

What Ericsson and Simon specifically propose is that verbalisations reflect at least part of the contents of verbal short-term memory (STM), a term which they use in a similar way to "working memory" as discussed in Chapter Two. These in turn reflect the information which is heeded or attended to by the subject at a given time. If the controversial product/process distinction is accepted, they are saying in effect that the (conscious?) products are being recorded in STM from which the underlying processes might be inferred. This is particularly helpful in tracing thought processes extended in time and producing a number of intermediate products. A good example is the solution of cryptarithmetic problems discussed at length by Newell and Simon (1972).

Ericsson and Simon (1980; 1984) present an information processing theory of cognition which attempts to explain how and why verbal reports are produced and consequently provides pointers to how they should be interpreted. It is not necessary to consider this theory in detail here, but it is interesting to note the conditions under which they expect verbal reports to be more or less informative. They regard probing techniques which are retrospective or inviting subjects to theorise about their behaviour as poor methods. Hence, they are not surprised by the poor self-knowledge demonstrated in the studies Nisbett and Wilson discuss. They also suggest that verbal reports will be most useful when the information would have been encoded in verbal STM anyway. Verbalisation which requires subjects to recode information from a non-visual form or which requires them to engage in additional cognitive activity is more problematical.

Ericsson and Simon (1984, Chapter Three) also address the incompleteness problem in depth. When will important information *not* be included in a verbal report? They identify two main types of processes which will not register: (1) control processes which have become "automated" due to over-learning and no longer register in STM (cf. Schneider & Shiffrin, 1977; Shiffrin & Schneider, 1977); and (2) recognition processes responsible for rapid retrieval of information from long- to short-term memory. In fact, they use the concept of recognition processes to explain two of the areas in which poor metacognition has been demonstrated in the empirical review section of this chapter. Intuitive judgement is classed as such a recognition process. Hence, they explain poor confidence ratings of judgements on the grounds that "…without any direct evidence from the process of retrieval confidence cannot be judged". Similarly, in discussing the Wason and Evans findings of false strategy reports in reasoning they suggest that matching bias reflects a recognition process and that it is only the requirement to produce a verbal justification which induces a more explicit form of reasoning. As they recognise, this is essentially similar to my own view that the "introspections" in fact reflect a *post hoc* reasoning process aimed at justifying a decision already taken.

CONCLUSIONS

We are now in a position to draw together the discussion of both the empirical and theoretical literature as it affects the issue of self-knowledge in reasoning. Because I have emphasised the preconscious nature of heuristic processes, there may be a temptation to equate the Evans (1984a) heuristic/analytic distinction with Broadbent's implicit/explicit division. This, however, would be erroneous. There are in fact—and as Ericsson and Simon recognise—two different types of processes which are not reflected in verbalisable knowledge. The first is what Evans (1984a) calls heuristic processes and what Ericsson and Simon call recognition processes. These are the preconscious and inaccessible processes by which the subject and focus of our attention is determined. Such processes are equally involved whether attention is directed towards sensory input or information retrieved from memory. The trick is to realise that what Evans (1984a) terms the "analytic" processes—those by which inferences are actually drawn—correspond to *both* types of control processes discussed by Reber, Broadbent and others. In other words they include implicit *and* explicit processes. Implicit processes correspond roughly to what Ericsson and Simon call "automatic" processes, except that the work reviewed earlier suggests that such processes may be acquired without *ever having been explicit*, and not simply become automated through overlearning. Whatever the origin, some high-level cognitive processes appear to operate in an implicit manner and are hence not verbalisable.

The original Wason and Evans dual process theory did not recognise the distinction between these two types of unconscious (for want of a better term) process so I should clarify my current explanation of the selection task behaviour. The cause of card choices in the selection task reflects—according to the arguments presented in this book—a preconscious heuristic judgement of relevance, probably linguistically determined. Subjects' verbal justifications and explanations, however, reflect an *explicit* analytic reasoning process in which subjects are able to justify their decisions in a manner which clearly recognises the logical relationships involved. The problem is that they could not apply this type of explicit verbal reasoning to solve the problem originally set. Subjects can analyse the relationships explicitly, but without prompting they do not do so.

Other reasoning tasks—such as transitive inference—clearly do induce some form of analytic reasoning, but not necessarily an explicit one. One is not entitled to assume that because reasoning is successful, then any verbal account offered by the subject must be accurate—hence, the mysterious reports of an "imagery strategy" in transitive inference which objective measures have failed to confirm. Retrospective reporting generally appears to produce new explicit reasoning from the subject who joins the experimenter in theorising about his behaviour, rather than a recollection of the method actually used. However, the use of concurrent verbalisation analysed for the locus of the subjects' attention, as advocated by Ericsson and Simon can be useful in the context of reasoning research, as Evans et al. (1983) have demonstrated.

What are the implications of all this for the understanding of biases in reasoning? We have seen in this book that reasoning and judgemental errors are very common in observed performance relative to the competence which people can be shown to possess. People can reason out the answer to syllogisms, for example, but frequently fall prey to a syntactic or semantic source of bias. Intuitive statistical judgements can, under favourable conditions, take heed of the law of large numbers or even base rates, but all too often fail to do so. People understand the logic of falsification of hypotheses but often cannot find the appropriate strategy to achieve this, even when exhorted by instructions. People understand the essential truth conditions of conditional sentences but cannot apply this knowledge to solution of the selection task.

The issues discussed in this chapter are, in my view, crucial to understanding the problem of biases. Explicit understanding of the logical essentials of a task does not guarantee successful reasoning and freedom from bias. Much of our thinking is intuitive, implicit, heuristic even when applied to explicitly defined problems. Biases are able to flourish because we are so little aware of the nature of our thinking or at least of crucial steps in it. The second aspect of defective self-knowledge is critical also. Despite all the philosophical arguments, the evidence is clear that we often hold false beliefs about our own cognitive processes. In most cases, these false beliefs are self-flattering. We are convinced of the rationality of our reasoning, highly adept at constructing plausible explanations for our decision behaviour, too confident that our judgements are correct, convinced that we could have predicted uncertain matters after the event, and so on. The origins of reasoning biases have been discussed in previous chapters. The combination of limited access and delusory rationality discussed in this chapter helps to explain why they are so persistent.

6 Implications and Applications

The purpose of the preceding chapters has been to convey an understanding of the range and nature of biases observed in experimental studies of human reasoning and to discuss their likely causes. The object of this final chapter is to consider the practical implications of this work and to discuss—in rather speculative vein—the ways in which we might limit the potential damage that such biases inflict on real life thinking and decision making. First, however, it is necessary to draw together some general conclusions emerging from the discussion to date.

THE NATURE OF REASONING BIASES

As I said at the outset of this book, human beings are profoundly intelligent in a sense which is proving extremely difficult to emulate in computer programs designed to exhibit artificial intelligence. The view that I wish to argue here is that errors of thinking occur because of, rather than in spite of, the nature of our intelligence. In other words, they are an inevitable consequence of the way in which we think and a price to be paid for the extraordinary effectiveness with which we routinely deal with the massive information processing requirements of everyday life.

The early attempts of Newell and Simon (1972) to simulate human problem solving in intelligent computer programs led to two major insights of relevance here. First of all, it was realised that we think not about the world but about a *mental representation of the world*. The same external world situation which constitutes the "problem" can be represented in many different ways, and the adequacy of the representation actually constructed may crucially affect the success of the problem solving which follows. Secondly, it was realised that any non-trivial problem involves searching through a vast range of alternative possible solution paths. Such a search could not be performed exhaustively but must perforce require the development of selective processing strategies capable of achieving solutions in a realistic time, but liable to failure.

The human being, viewed as an information processing system, faces a massive problem of information reduction. Both the formation and manipulation of mental representations must be carried out in a highly selective manner using some form of heuristic process. We must similarly have intelligent, selective search strategies for retrieving from our vast memories of factual and procedural knowledge just those items relevant to the problem at hand. It is little surprising that such a system is vulnerable to bias and error.

A number of the phenomena discussed in this book are generally consistent with the argument expressed above. People frequently are able to show understanding of a logical or statistical principle in one situation and appear to ignore it altogether in another. Specific arguments have been advanced for the effects reviewed to show, in general, how some form of selective processing was responsible. For example, a bias to represent and think about information in a positive rather than negative manner was shown to explain the results of many "confirmation bias" experiments as well as the well-established matching bias in conditional reasoning. Similarly, belief bias in deductive reasoning was shown to be consistent with a model in which arguments are selectively scrutinised according to the acceptability of their conclusions. One can even argue that such biases are adaptive in a system faced with a major information reduction problem. For example, why devote precious cognitive resources to evaluating the evidence for a statement already known or assumed to be true?

One type of bias, then, consists of failure to apply a principle which is understood—a good example being provided by the Wason selection task. Although we know that subjects have a reasonable understanding of the truth conditions of a conditional statement, they consistently fail to formulate an effective strategy for testing them on the standard version of the problem. On this task, as on the 2 4 6 and similar problems, subjects can recognise and correctly utilise falsifying evidence should they be presented with it, but have great difficulty in finding such evidence for themselves. However, in other cases—particularly with regard to statistical inferences—it appears that biases may reflect defective understanding of the principles involved. For example, base rate data is generally ignored even though it is highly salient and available in the problem presentation, subjects erroneously believe that the value of a sample relates to the size of the population from which it is drawn, and people appear to have a defective understanding of the diagnosticity of evidence.

The discussion of self-knowledge in Chapter Five is consistent with the selective processing account of many of the biases discussed in this book. Here it was argued that much complex thinking occurs at an unconscious, implicit level and that far from revealing the underlying strategies, verbal reports of reasoning can be misleading rationalisations. Since pre-attentive processes which determine the locus of attention must of necessity be unconscious it is to be expected that key processes in information reduction will be inaccessible to verbal report. However, the work discussed carries the further implication that people may well be unaware of the fact that their decisions are subject to bias and adept at constructing rational sounding explanations after the event. This, in turn, could lead to resistance to the notion that any debiasing is necessary.

APPROACHES TO DEBIASING

I shall use the term "debiasing" here to refer to the problem of how to reduce or eliminate the impact of biases in reasoning, decision making, and problem solving. I shall discuss several alternative approaches to this problem, in the light of the theoretical perspective provided by the preceding discussion of psychological research on the nature of biases. The approaches are: (1) replacement of the human intuitions by a formal procedure; (2) education and training to improve reasoning ability; (3) improving the design of the environment in which the human operates; and (4) the development of interactive decision aids.

Replacement Approaches

The notion that human cognition should be replaced partially or completely by a formal system—usually a computer program—has already received a partial acceptance in modern society. For example, there is widespread agreement that computers are better suited than humans to the task of accurate storage and retrieval of well-defined information and the computerised database is already an indispensable part of modern life. No longer does an insurance broker need to try to guess or remember which company will offer the cheapest premium for the particular circumstances of a customer—a computer program will find the answer reliably and quickly when supplied with the relevant data. We are also quite happy to let computers perform lengthy—but again well-defined computations. Who would nowadays perform a complex statistical analysis by hand? Computers used in this way are seen simply as powerful tools under full control of their human masters.

The problems arise, however, when intelligent thought or judgemental decision making are involved—precisely the kinds of task with which this book is concerned. The problems are of two kinds—technical and social.

The technical problems arise because computer programs are not really that smart yet, for all the efforts of the artificial intelligence researchers. There has, of course, been a recent vogue for building "expert systems" (cf. Hayes-Roth, Waterman, & Lenat, 1983)—computer programs which aim to emulate the reasoning of human experts. The discipline of "knowledge engineering" has developed with the aim of extracting knowledge from human experts and programming it into a computer. This has proved very difficult because a vast amount of knowledge is involved in solving a real world problem, and procedural knowledge is particularly hard to elicit by interview methods (see Chapter Five and Evans, 1988 for discussion of this point). In practice, the few expert systems that have been of practical value have been directed to very limited and well-defined problem domains such as diagnosis of particular types of medical disorder.

At present, full replacement of human judgement in the solution of complex and ill-defined problems—e.g., most aspects of governmental decision making—is impractical on technical grounds. Even if it were not, it is likely that there would be enormous social resistance to the idea of computers making important decisions. Hence, I do not see any realistic prospect of the replacement of complex human reasoning and decision making by intelligent computer programs on more than a very limited scale in the foreseeable future. The development of interactive decision aids which work *with* a human being are, however, a much more promising line which I will discuss in some detail later in the chapter. Such approaches may involve a partial replacement of processes otherwise left to intuition, as we shall see.

Education and Training

Perhaps the most obvious response to the problem is try to devise methods of education and training of individuals to improve their reasoning. There are a number of theoretical considerations arising from the discussions in the book which are relevant to this approach. For example, the effectiveness of such training may well depend upon the nature of the bias. It was noted above that in some cases biases arise because subjects fail to apply understanding of a principle which they possess. In this case, reinforcing the teaching of the theory involved is not likely to be helpful. Biases which reflect faulty understanding of the underlying principles should be much more amenable.

A second general issue concerns the generality or specificity of approaches to teaching thinking. The general view amongst psychologists and educationalists interested in the problem appears to be that it is possible to teach critical thinking as a general skill (see Nickerson, Perkins, & Smith, 1985; Baron, 1985). However, the evidence reviewed in this book must cast doubt upon this assumption. First of all, most of the experiments reported have been conducted on college students who have been exposed to a good deal of education which should have developed their general ability to think to at least a reasonable extent—and yet we see the very high rates of errors and biases on the experimental tasks presented. Secondly, we have seen that the ability to solve the problems given is affected dramatically by a whole range of presentation and content factors. Furthermore, in some of my own work I have specifically examined individual differences in deductive reasoning to see whether correlations exist on the basis of understanding a logical principle and failed to find such a pattern (e.g., Evans, 1977; Pollard & Evans, 1980). Taken together, these findings suggest that error patterns are determined far more strongly by the characteristics of the task than by any general factor of reasoning ability that the individual subject brings to it. I will return to this point later.

The other main implication from the psychological literature on reasoning concerns the role of verbal thinking and the effectiveness of verbal instruction. This is, of course, the most widely used educational method but there is good reason to believe that it will be largely ineffective in the teaching of reasoning skills. There is a good deal of evidence to support this view which has already been presented in different parts of this book. Much of the indirect evidence and theoretical arguments considered in Chapter Five support the notion that the processes underlying complex reasoning tasks are largely non-verbal, intuitive and implicit. Since verbal instruction presumably has its major impact on verbal and explicit thought processes, one might well expect that formal instruction in logical principles and so on will not prove very effective. A number of experimental studies already reviewed in this book appear to support this conclusion.

In Chapter Three, various studies were discussed in which the authors attempted to remove confirmation bias by use of instructional manipulations. Most of the experiments involved explanation of the principles involved, stressing the importance of falsification, testing of alternative strategies, etc. These attempts were singularly unsuccessful and the one apparent exception reported by Gorman and Gorman (1984) was shown to be due to the subjects being directly instructed to make negative tests of their prediction. In fact, the most effective debiasing manipulation in the confirmation bias literature has been the DAX and MED experiment of Tweney et al. (1980), described in the chapter, which appears to overcome the positivity bias by providing a positive label for what is normally seen as a negated alternative. This literature provides strong support for the argument that a selective processing bias, rather than a lack of conceptual understanding, is responsible for the errors observed. A similar conclusion is warranted by the findings of Barston (1986), noted in Chapter Four, on a deductive reasoning task. She ran a whole series of experiments on syllogistic reasoning with very detailed elaboration of the principle of logical necessity provided in the instructions. Very little facilitation of logical reasoning performance was observed and the belief bias effect remained. This is again quite consistent with the explanation of belief bias—reflecting preconscious heuristic processes—offered in the chapter.

The most extensive study of instructional training on the Wason selection task is that reported by Cheng, Holyoak, Nisbett, and Oliver (1986), mentioned briefly in Chapter Four but worthy of closer examination here. In the first experiment reported, subjects were given either rule- or example-based training, both or neither. The former included detailed instruction on the logic of conditionals followed by an inference exercise with feedback. The examples training involved presentation of two examples, including the D'Andrade Sears problem (see Table 4.3), together with the correct solution but no explanation. As predicted by their pragmatic reasoning schema theory (cf. Cheng & Holyoak, 1985, discussed in Chapter Four) neither form of training was effective in itself in facilitating performance on a subsequent selection task, although the combination of the two was successful. The second experiment in the paper involved an examination of the effect of a semester of formal training in standard logic with pre- and post-tests of selection task performance. No improvement in performance on the task was observed. The final experiment in the paper showed that training subjects in the use of an "obligation schema"—whose prescriptions map on to those of formal logic—had a marked effect on the solution of subsequent selection tasks which lent themselves to interpretation within this schema.

The Cheng et al. study, as the authors conclude, suggests that performance on the Wason selection task does not reflect understanding of abstract logical principles and that formal instruction, even at a set of logic classes, is of little help. These conclusions are compatible with those already made above, although a couple of somewhat discrepant results in the literature should be noted. Hoch and Tschirgi (1985) compared bachelors and masters students and found a significantly higher level of reasoning performance with the latter group. This suggests that a factor of general reasoning ability is operating, although this is the only finding of this kind of which I am aware in the long history of the selection task literature. The second paper which appears to spoil the story a little is that of Berry (1983). In line with a number of previous studies she found that presentation of a concrete selection task problem did not in itself facilitate performance on a later abstract one, but when combined with instructions to verbalise while solving the concrete problem, a significant facilitation on the abstract problem was observed. However, I know of no successful replications of Berry's findings and there is at least one report of a failure to replicate these verbalisation effects (see Chrostowski & Griggs, 1985).

On the whole, there is very little evidence that deductive reasoning biases can be removed by verbal instruction relating to the underlying logical principles. Recent evidence suggests, however, that the picture may be rather different in the case of statistical reasoning. As mentioned in Chapter Four, Fong, Krantz, and Nisbett (1986) reported a study of statistical inference with a similar design to that of Cheng et al. described above, but with strikingly different results. In this case, experimental training of either a rule- or an example-based nature proved effective in either case in facilitating the use of the statistical law of large numbers on subsequent problem solving. The second contrast with the Cheng et al. study was the finding that attendance at formal statistics classes also produced a marked improvement in performance on the experimental problems. This has led the related group of authors to the rather uncomfortable conclusion that statistical, but not logical reasoning may be based upon general rules (cf. Holland et al., 1986, discussed in my Chapter Four).

The discrepancy between the instructional training effects on the two types of reasoning is consistent with some observations already made in this book. In the case of the selection task, and the other reasoning problems discussed on which instructions have been ineffective, a clear argument was made in each case for the bias arising from selective heuristic processes in the identification of "relevant" problem features. The review of the law of large numbers in Chapter Two, however, led rather to the conclusion that subjects have a fragile intuition about this, albeit vulnerable to over-complicated instructions or the presence of more salient competing variables. It was also observed earlier in this chapter that in the case of statistical reasoning, errors often appeared to reflect defective understanding—as opposed to non-application—of the principles involved.

It is important to consider experience-based training as an alternative to instructional training, especially since this may be more effective in developing implicit thought processes. Indeed, the studies by Reber, Broadbent and others reviewed in Chapter Five show precisely that effective procedural knowledge may be acquired at an implicit level by asking subjects to make judgements and then providing effective feedback. There are few studies of experience-based training reported in the reasoning literature but I will consider one example here. In Chapter Five, I provided a brief discussion of the literature on overconfidence in which subjects generally provide over-optimistic probability estimates in judging the likelihood that they have answered questions correctly. Such subjects were said to be poorly "calibrated". Lichtenstein and Fischhoff (1980) reported a study in which an attempt was made to improve calibration on general knowledge questions by use of feedback training.

Feedback on probability judgements is tricky, since unless a prediction is made with a likelihood of 0 or 1, then no single outcome can disprove the forecast. Indeed, this may be one of the reasons that people do not appear to develop good intuitions about probability through real life experience of risky events. In Chapter Five, it was suggested that the reason that weather forecasters were found to be well calibrated was precisely because they received accurate and frequent feedback on a large number of related predictions. Lichtenstein and Fischhoff managed to provide a laboratory simulation of this kind of feedback by providing a summary of results after each block of 200 trials. The findings were encouraging to the extent that subjects who were not well calibrated to start with improved significantly as a result of the training. However, little transfer was observed to a second task involving question answering in a different domain.

Transfer of training between one domain and another is an important problem in all these studies, as is the duration of the benefits which any training might impart. Unfortunately, it appears that the two may interact. Fong et al. (1986) found that the benefits of their experimental training transferred to a problem domain different from that in which the training occurred. Unfortunately, a subsequent study by Fong and Nisbett (described by Holland et al., 1986) led to the observation that such transfer was present only on an immediate and not a delayed test, although benefit was retained for problems in the domain of training.

My recommendations on approaches to debiasing by training are based upon the theoretical analysis of reasoning biases given in this book and upon the relatively few studies which have directly aimed to correct such biases which have been discussed in this section. First of all I do not see much theoretical interest in instructing subjects in strategies specific to the task as was done by Gorman and Gorman (1984) or in a recent study of statistical reasoning reported by Lopes (1987). However, such instruction could possibly be beneficial in an applied context where a limited and explicitly known set of strategies are applicable. I am sceptical of the view that thinking can be taught as a general skill and it is quite clear that verbal instruction in general principles of reasoning is unlikely, in itself, to provide protection from biases arising in specific situations. Hence, I would like to see an expansion of efforts to provide training which is both experience-based and in the domain of application. The aim should be to replace faulty intuitions with more accurate ones whilst still operating at the level of implicit thought processes.

In this regard, I see a great potential for the development of training software which uses the power of the computer to simulate the experience of operating in a given domain. As an example, in my own current research I am interested in improving the intuitions that psychology students (and staff!) hold about probability in order to improve the effectiveness of their research design decisions. In particular, I am interested in subjective understanding of the power of research designs which is affected by several variables such as sample size, effect size, and significance level. In order to acquire an accurate intuitive feel for the problem, people need to have repeated experience of the soundness of their decisions. The problem is that real life does not provide it, even for experienced researchers, since in practice one does not know whether an effect is present, and if so how big it is, and the feedback provided by real experiments comes in any case at far too infrequent intervals.

Hence, I have developed training software which provides on-line graphical simulations of the sampling distributions associated with different parameter values in the hope that users will develop an intuitive grasp of the effects of their decisions (see Fig. 6.1). Users of the program are told (or can set for themselves) the value of several parameters which affect the power characteristics of an experiment using the binomial test. These parameters are the significance level, the size of the sample and the effect size. For example, for the problem illustrated in Fig. 6.1 the significance level is 5%, the sample size 200 and the effect size indicated by the information that the population being sampled is really 55–45 as opposed to the 50–50 null hypothesis specified. The subject is asked to guess or estimate the chance of such an experiment providing a significant result. The program then runs a Monte Carlo simulation in which results of successive experiments are plotted in a histogram on the screen. This takes several seconds with regular screen updates so that a picture of the process is built up over time. A solid vertical line is drawn at the critical value required for a significant result. Hence, in the diagram, the proportion of the distribution to the right of this line provides a visual indication of the power probability or percentage of significant results. Only after the display is complete is the computed theoretical power probability printed on the screen, in case of sampling error in the empirical result.

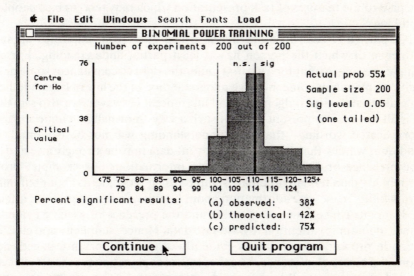

FIG. 6.1. Example computer screen illustrating on-line graphical simulation software of the sampling distributions associated with different parameter values.

Of course, a much simpler procedure to program would have involved simply giving people numerical feedback of the actual power probability. However, I do not believe that just providing numbers would help people to understand the process of sampling and the relationships between the three parameters involved. The object of the graphical displays is to help users develop an effective mental model of the sampling process. This in turn should help them to run mental simulations when confronted with new situations and greatly enhance the accuracy of their statistical intuitions. At the time of writing, the software is complete but I have not yet had the opportunity to run evaluation studies to determine its effectiveness. However, I hope that discussion of this example has illustrated the kind of approach to training which I favour.

The Task Environment

The experimental studies reviewed in the earlier chapters of this book have illustrated how a range of features of the presentation of tasks may affect the susceptibility of subjects to error and bias. Hence, another approach to debiasing concerns the design of environments in which people will be required to reason and make decisions. Opportunity for such design arises in a variety of situations such as: (a) the framing of rules and regulations which need to be understood by the general public; (b) the development of educational material to optimise understanding of ideas and principles; and (c) the design of interactive computer environments for access to information used in decision making. In particular, the burgeoning field of user interface design (see, for example, Norman & Draper, 1986) is one in which attention should be paid to the features of task presentation which may tend to bias people's thinking.

Of particular relevance are biases which arise from failure to apply a principle of which the person has at least partial understanding. For example, we saw in Chapter Two that under the right circumstances some or all subjects may show some intuitive understanding of the law of large numbers in making statistical judgements and inferences. However, we also saw that it is all too easy to present tasks in such a way—normally by unnecessarily complicated wording—that such understanding will not be exhibited. In addition, we saw that attention to relevant data may be strongly affected by the presence or absence of competing information. For example, proportionality data tend to dominate sample size in judgements about binomial probability; irrelevant information about population size, if present, affects judgements concerning sample size; and the presence of specific evidence tends to minimise attention to base rate data. Hence, simplicity and clarification in presentation of data is evidently of great importance in reducing potential errors of inference. The theoretical explanation for the effects described above may well lie in considerations of cognitive constraints, particularly of attention span and working memory capacity, and studies were considered in earlier chapters which directly implicated such constraints on processing capacity in the production of inferential errors.

The studies of abstract conditional reasoning and of confirmation bias discussed in Chapters Two and Three demonstrate a very clear and general positivity bias in human reasoning. People evidently have great difficulty in thinking about information which is encoded either linguistically or logically in a negative form. The dramatic scope for debiasing in this regard is shown by studies which have used tasks so designed as to permit people to form positive mental representations of features that would normally be encoded negatively (e.g., Tweney et al., 1980; Griggs & Newstead, 1982). Clearly this is a matter which should be given close attention in the framing of instructional material, rules and regulations, and the like.

It is less clear, in the light of the conclusions of Chapter Three, whether there is a "confirmation bias" in the form of a motivational tendency to maintain beliefs, despite the importance attached to this phenomenon by authors such as Baron (1985). There is, of course, evidence from studies in cognitive social psychology (see Nisbett & Ross, 1980) that people do tend to avoid or discredit evidence which conflicts with strongly held beliefs. Taken in conjunction with the clear evidence of belief bias discussed in Chapter Four, it does appear that preconceived attitudes are likely to prejudice the construction and evaluation of arguments in various ways. It is important in this regard to recognise the asymmetry involved in the belief bias effect and the theoretical explanation which was proposed to account for it in Chapter Four. What the Selective Scrutiny model (cf. Barston, 1986) actually proposes is that people are much more likely to scrutinise the arguments for a conclusion which conflicts with prior belief.

What this means in practice is that people will tend to accept uncritically any argument or evidence which supports an existing belief—as in Lord, Ross, and Lepper's (1979) study of peoples' assessments of studies arguing for and against capital punishment. The scrutiny of arguments with unbelievable conclusions does, however, sometimes lead to appreciation that they are valid (cf. Evans, Barston, & Pollard, 1983). This perhaps has implications for design of educational material in that the use of arguments expressing controversial or surprising viewpoints will be more likely to stimulate active thought. More depressingly, it provides encouragement for those more interested in indoctrination than education. Preaching to the converted, it would appear, requires little skill of argument.

One of the most important debiasing factors in reasoning also relates to problem content as discussed in the latter part of Chapter Four. The detailed history of study of content effects on the Wason selection task has led to some fairly clear theoretical conclusions, albeit generalised primarily from work on one particular paradigm. It certainly appears that effective reasoning learned in one type of situation can be transferred under the right conditions to another, whether or not one accepts the theory of pragmatic reasoning schemas favoured in some of the recent work. In particular, it appears that good reasoning may result from the successful identification of analogies between the problem at hand and previous situations, the properties of which have been learned by experience. The use of effective semantic content may also remove altogether the influence of biases such as matching which arise from the syntactic structure of verbal problems. There is little doubt that the use of abstract or arbitrary terms inhibits good reasoning, even amongst the higher than average intelligence groups normally used in the laboratory experiments. As many a teacher knows already from experience, concrete examples and well formed analogies are of great importance in communicating new ideas.

In this section I have discussed briefly the main types of factor in the task presentation and environment which are likely to increase or reduce biased reasoning. Such considerations can help to guide thinking about the design of any specific environment but are not a substitute for psychological study in a given application. In particular, there has been a rapid development of computer-based information systems which are playing an ever increasing role in human decision making. The way in which such information is structured in the data base or presented on the screen may have possibly profound effects for better or worse on the way in which the user thinks about the problem environment. The development of such systems, largely in the absence of any study of their psychological characteristics, must give cause for concern and the recent emergence of serious psychological thought about this problem is most welcome (cf. Norman & Draper, 1986).

Interactive Decision Aids

The positive aspect of the development of computerised working environments is that they provide the opportunity in themselves for active debiasing to be attempted. Earlier in the chapter I said that I saw only a limited role at present for the development of expert system programs to replace human beings in the making of decisions and solving of problems. However, I see great scope for computer systems working with human experts in order to produce more effective decisions than could be made by either a person or a machine working separately. Before describing the principles on which I feel such interactive decision aids should be based, it is first necessary to note some developments in this direction from the decision analysis tradition.

As mentioned in Chapter One, decision analysis is concerned with the problem of helping humans to make effective decisions by application of prescriptive decision theory, and has been practised by some psychologists for many years (see von Winterfeldt & Edwards, 1986). The analyst will first attempt to help decision makers structure their problems and subsequently try to evaluate the structure and recommend an optimal choice by using formal decision theory. The structuring process often involves construction of a decision tree, in which an initial set of alternative actions available to the decision maker is associated with alternative events or outcomes with associated probabilities. The tree may be grown by consideration of further possible actions that may be taken after each event with evaluation of the consequences of those actions and so on. The tree is pruned to some reasonable size which lends itself to clear understanding by the decision maker and then estimated values or utilities are attached to the final outcomes. Optimal choices may then be made by use of such principles as dominance and maximisation of expected value. However, the psychologists involved in this field appear to regard the problem structuring itself as providing the major benefit (cf. Humphreys & McFadden, 1980; Berkeley & Humphreys, 1982; von Winterfeldt & Edwards, 1986).

Decision analysis is not a response to the evidence of bias in reasoning, since it was well established before the work of psychologists like Kahneman and Tversky got going. Reactions of psychologists in the older tradition of studying decision making to the "heuristics and biases" work appear to range from indifference (Phillips, 1987) through bewilderment (von Winterfeldt & Edwards, 1986, Chapter 13) to outright hostility (Berkeley & Humphreys, 1982; Christensen-Szalanski & Beach, 1984). Nevertheless, it is possible to view decision analysis as a debiasing method and to consider its potential application to the development of interactive decision aids. The strength of problem structuring, noted by its proponents, may be seen to arise from the fact that people are helped to develop effective mental models of the problem and to compensate for working memory limitations by externalising these in the form of diagrams such as decision trees. The use of formal decision theory to recommend choices between actions also appears preferable to wholistic, intuitive judgements where unconscious biases may flourish.

Decision analysis does not, however, provide complete protection from biases, which probably accounts for some of the hostile reactions of its advocates to recent experimental work on reasoning. In particular, the Bayesian approach taken assumes that probability is a subjective concept of confidence which can be rationally determined by the individual. The mass of evidence of irrationality in probability judgement, much of which has been discussed in this book, may thus be seen as a challenge to the fundamental philosophy of this approach. From the point of view of developing interactive decision aids, there is also a problem with the sheer complexity of conventional decision analysis which has been practised as more of an art than a science, involving very flexible approaches to structuring which in themselves depend upon detailed human understanding of the problem domain.

In spite of these difficulties an attempt has been made to provide automated decision analysis by Pat Humphreys and colleagues (see, for example, Humphreys & Wishuda, 1981; Humphreys & McFadden, 1980). The program, called MAUD (Multi-Attribute Utility Decomposition), has gone through various versions but the general principle of its application is unchanged. The program develops a relatively simple two dimensional matrix structure which plots alternative actions against a set of aspects or attributes relevant to their evaluation. For example, if the actions were to buy alternative makes of car, the aspects might be such dimensions as cost, style, engine power, passenger space, and so on. Once a problem is structured in this manner, each action may be evaluated on each aspect and the optimal choice prescribed by application of "multi-attribute utility" theory (see, for example, Edwards, 1977).

MAUD incorporates some psychological techniques, for example by using the repertory grid method of George Kelly (1955) to elicit names of alternative dimensions, and by using indirect methods to determine the relative weighting which subjects attach to different aspects. It also performs correlations on the matrix of values produced in order to test for the inclusion of two or more identical aspects under different names which can distort the computation of an optimal decision. An independent evaluation of MAUD3 was recently reported by John, von Winterfeldt, and Edwards (1983) who presented the program to one group, and a human decision analysis to another. They generally found a close convergence between the human and automated decision analyses, and, despite some specific criticisms of the MAUD program, made a favourable conclusion with regard to the development of stand-alone analysis aids.

The approach taken by MAUD stands in stark contrast to expert consultant systems. First of all, it is entirely empty of any domain knowledge. By contrast, an expert system has a large amount of detailed knowledge of a given domain and is able to understand and utilise data about particular cases provided by the user. The primary aim of MAUD is to enable users to structure their problems in an appropriate manner and the secondary aim is to recommend (only) decisions by application of formal decision theory. By contrast the expert system, having elicited the relevant data from the user, then proceeds to reason out a solution to the problem itself. The difference between these two approaches reflects the kind of human consultant on which each is modelled. A decision analyst helps someone use their own knowledge of a problem to solve it, whereas an expert system mimics the kind of consultant, such as a medical or legal expert, whom you request to solve a problem on your behalf.

There is, I believe, much scope for decision support systems which fall between these extremes. On the one hand, I am doubtful of the value of a computer program which has no knowledge of the domain and no kind of intelligence such as MAUD, but on the other hand I feel it unrealistic and unnecessary to expect a program to be able to entirely replace the human being. I suggest that an interactive decision aid should be capable of performing at least some of the following functions: (1) provision—where possible—of databases of well-defined factual information so as to inform aspects of the decision; (2) provision of computational procedures to assist the user in calculating the consequences of possible decisions; (3) methods of structuring the problem and representing its essential characteristics in a comprehensible form to the user; and (4) use of decision theory to recommend optimal decisions.

A system of this kind provides scope for debiasing decision making in several respects. The provision of relevant and accurate information—together with prompting of when it is appropriate to consult such a database—helps to avoid errors arising from ignorance, laziness, insufficient access to or search of published sources, and so on. Computational procedures which replace intuitive judgements can obviously reduce bias. The modelling of the decision process and representation of the problem to the user reduces the chance of the user losing track due to working memory limitations or poor organisation, and finally the decision theory provides a rational basis for final choices.

At the time of writing, I am engaged in a collaborative research project with Ian Dennis and Lakshmi Sastry in which an interactive decision aid incorporating all of these principles is being developed. The system is designed to assist psychologists and others in the choice of design characteristics for experimental research involving statistical measurement. The system guides people through a series of decisions helping them to structure the problem as a database of alternative design scenarios. Decisions are aided by providing information about available statistical tests, performing formal power calculations to replace intuitive judgements, and recommending optimal choices both within and between alternative design scenarios by the use of decision theory. At the time of writing the system is fully designed in principle but the program code is only partially implemented and tested. A detailed preliminary report on the design and implementation details of the system is provided by Evans, Dennis, and Sastry (1988).

SOME FINAL THOUGHTS

The task of the psychologist is to understand behaviour, not to judge it. That is why I expressed a rather cool attitude to the debate about human rationality which has impinged recently on the field, when discussing this problem in Chapter One. However, psychologists interested in reasoning and judgement cannot evade the issue entirely. There is an increasing recognition by engineers, computer scientists, and others that human cognitive processes, especially those of the highest level, are a critical factor in the design of any system involving human beings. Moreover they expect—quite reasonably—that psychologists should be able to offer both theoretical understanding and methodological tools to assist them in dealing with the problems they face. An essential consideration in such an exercise is the nature of cognitive constraints which will limit the effectiveness of human performance unless understood, and compensated for, by the system.

The psychology of reasoning involves addressing two major types of theoretical question: (1) by what mechanism is reasoning competence achieved; and (2) by what means, and under what conditions, is reasoning performance constrained? A complete theory must deal with both these questions since the behaviour we will observe will reflect both underlying competence and performance factors. There are, however, different emphases placed on these questions by different authors. A number of rival theorists are currently attempting to demonstrate their own view of competence whilst, in some cases, providing minimal reference to evidence of performance factors. By contrast, in this book, I have given detailed attention to the understanding of limitations in performance whilst remaining largely neutral on the question of the mechanisms responsible for the effective reasoning which is also—and undeniably—exhibited. In so doing, I have attempted to use such terms as "error" and "bias" in as clear and uncontroversial a manner as possible. The consideration is not whether the behaviour conforms narrowly to standard logic but whether or not a person reasoning in a particular manner could be expected to make effective and successful decisions.

In general, theory and application in psychology have remained uncomfortably separated. Theoretical research can become self-sustaining as the scientists involved argue about ever more detailed issues related to the experimental paradigms themselves, and lose sight of the broader questions which motivated the work originally. Sometimes, pursuit of a paradigm can lead to understanding of important issues that were not involved at the outset. An excellent example, demonstrated in the course of this book, is that of the Wason selection task which was originally presented as a (suspect) demonstration of confirmation bias, but which has become a major vehicle for the understanding of the influence of knowledge on reasoning. A less appealing history is offered by that of reasoning with classical syllogisms which, while producing some discussion of important general issues (e.g., belief bias, mental models), has also generated a proliferation of theories and models concerned more with the task itself than the general nature of the mental processes involved in reasoning.

Applied research, on the other hand, is all too often pursued in the absence of good theory—perhaps by those wishing to address important real world problems and unwilling to await the results of the niggling debates of the theorists. However, recently—and importantly—a distinctive field of applied cognitive psychology has been emerging in which a number of cognitive psychologists have considered the application of their theoretical interests to practical problems. This seems to me to offer great potential benefit to the development of theory as well as to the solution of applied problems, since it broadens the nature of the empirical testing and also focuses the attention of researchers on wider questions. Cognitive science should support a discipline of cognitive engineering or the status of the science itself is in question.

It is for this reason that I have attempted to draw conclusions in this final chapter about the implications of the study of reasoning biases for applied issues and in particular the problem of debiasing. In doing so, however, I am aware of the difficulty of generalising from imperfect theory to a huge range of possible domains of application, each of which may have important individual and special features. Even in the more precise and better understood world of the physical sciences, matters are not that simple. The solution of practical engineering problems—so I am assured by my colleagues in such fields—is only partially facilitated by an understanding of the basic science. Why else do engineers still build computer and physical models to test the properties of their particular designs?

The applied cognitive psychologist must then make a detailed study of both the domain of application and the behaviour of individual people who work in the domain. The value of theory is largely heuristic in that it suggests appropriate questions to ask and methodologies to employ, and helps us to understand the data we collect. We cannot know, in advance of study, what biases may afflict the reasoning of people operating in a particular domain. It is, however, of great assistance to approach such a problem with examples of prior knowledge like the following: (a) verbal understanding of principles does not ensure their application in a given act of reasoning; (b) limitations of attention or working memory may lead people to ignore information in some circumstances which they would otherwise regard as relevant; (c) decisions may be based on implicit reasoning which cannot be articulated; (d) expert domain knowledge can have inhibitory and biasing influences on reasoning as well as the more obvious facilitatory effects; and (e) people may possess and apply inaccurate intuitions—for example concerning probability—which can persist even amongst those of considerable experience and expertise, and so on, and so forth.

Although some general ideas about debiasing have been discussed in this chapter, it is obvious that the best first approach in a given domain of application is to study the type of thinking involved and to identify the particular biases concerned. Even when armed with the kind of theoretical ideas outlined above and discussed in detail in this book, however, this is no simple task as I have discovered from recent personal experience. The most difficult assignment I have experienced as a psychologist is that involved in a current research project in which, together with other colleagues, I am attempting to understand the cognitive processes involved in engineering design. No one—least of all engineers—appears to have any real understanding at present of the nature of such design processes. You cannot even begin to apply theoretical knowledge until you have at least decided what kind of thinking—problem-solving, reasoning, decision processes?—is involved. Even as hardened experimentalists, we could see no initial alternative to the conduct of essentially descriptive, observational studies using methods such as protocol analysis. Nor is there any guarantee that the belief—widely held by engineers—that design is a general process is necessarily correct. It may well turn out to be heavily dependent upon both the domain of the design and the cognitive style of the individual engineer.

I concluded an earlier book on reasoning (Evans, 1982) with the hope that reasoning research would become better integrated theoretically with mainstream cognitive psychology. Even in the relatively short time that has elapsed since, significant progress has been made in this direction. In particular, the subsequent emergence—or at least flowering—of the semantic theories of reasoning by mental models, and by pragmatic reasoning schemas, have focused the attention of reasoning researchers, in line with other cognitive scientists, on *knowledge* as the central problem in the understanding of intelligence. Less productive, perhaps, has been the focus on the rationality debate during the 1980s with the attempts by some authors to deny or belittle the evidence of error and bias in human inference. My hope for the next decade is that applied cognitive psychology will continue to flourish on the basis of solid links with theoretical work. My belief is that the understanding of the constraints and limitations of higher cognitive processes has an important part to play in this endeavour.

References

Ajzen, I. (1977). Intuitive theories of events and the effects of base rate information on prediction. *Journal of Personality and Social Psychology*, *35*, 303–314.

Baddeley, A.D. (1986). *Working memory*. Oxford: Oxford University Press.

Baddeley, A.D. & Hitch, G.J. (1974). Working memory. In G.A. Bower (Ed.), *The psychology of learning and motivation*, *Vol. 8*. New York: Academic Press.

Bar-Hillel, M. (1979). The role of sample size in sample evaluation. *Organisational Behavior and Human Performance*, *24*, 245–257.

Bar-Hillel, M. (1980). The base-rate fallacy in probability judgements. *Acta Psychologica*, *44*, 211–233.

Baron, J. (1985). *Rationality and intelligence*. Cambridge: Cambridge University Press.

Barston, J.I. (1986). *An investigation into belief biases in reasoning*. Unpublished Ph.D. thesis, Plymouth Polytechnic.

Beach, L.R., Christensen-Szalanski, J., & Barnes, V. (1987). Assessing human judgement: Has it been done, can it be done, should it be done? In G. Wright & P. Ayton (Eds.), *Judgemental forecasting*. Chichester: Wiley.

Beattie, J. & Baron, J. (1988). Confirmation and matching biases in hypothesis testing. *Quarterly Journal of Experimental Psychology*, *40A*, 269–298.

Berkeley, D. & Humphreys, P. (1982). Structuring decision problems and the bias heuristic. *Acta Psychologica*, *50*, 201–252.

Berry, D.C. (1983). Metacognitive experience and transfer of logical reasoning. *Quarterly Journal of Experimental Psychology*, *35A*, 39–49.

Berry, D.C. & Broadbent, D.E. (1984). On the relationship between task performance and associated verbalizable knowledge. *Quarterly Journal of Experimental Psychology*, *36A*, 209–231.

Berry, D.C. & Broadbent, D.E. (1987). Explanation and verbalization in a computer assisted search task. *Quarterly Journal of Experimental Psychology*, *39A*, 585–609.

Beyth-Marom, R. & Arkes, H.R. (1983). Being accurate is not necessarily Bayesian—comments on Christensen-Szalanski and Beach. *Organisational Behavior and Human Performance*, *31*, 255–257.

Beyth-Marom, R. & Fischhoff, B. (1983). Diagnosticity and pseudodiagnosticity. *Journal of Personality and Social Psychology*, *45*, 1185–1197.

Bourne, L.E., Dominowski, R.L., & Loftus, E.F. (1979). *Cognitive processes*. Englewood Cliffs, N.J.: Prentice-Hall.

Braine, M.D.S. (1978). On the relation between the natural logic of reasoning and standard logic. *Psychological Review, 85*, 1–21.

Broadbent, D.E., Fitzgerald, P., & Broadbent, M.H.P. (1986). Implicit and explicit knowledge in the control of complex systems. *British Journal of Psychology, 77*, 33–50.

Brooks, L.R. (1978). Non-analytic concept formation and memory for instances. In E. Rosch & B.B. Lloyd (Eds.), *Cognition and categorisation*. Hillsdale, N.J.: Lawrence Erlbaum Associates Inc.

Brooks, P.G. (1984). *Visual and verbal processing in reasoning*. Unpublished Ph.D. thesis, Plymouth Polytechnic.

Chapman, L.J. & Chapman, J.P. (1959). Atmosphere effect re-examined. *Journal of Experimental Psychology, 58*, 220–226.

Chapman, L.J. & Chapman, J.P. (1967). Genesis of popular but erroneous psychodiagnostic observations. *Journal of Abnormal Psychology, 6*, 193–204.

Chapman, L.J. & Chapman, J.P. (1969). Illusory correlation as an obstacle to the use of valid diagnostic signs. *Journal of Abnormal Psychology, 74*, 271–280.

Cheng, P.W. & Holyoak, K.J. (1985). Pragmatic reasoning schemas. *Cognitive Psychology, 17*, 391–416.

Cheng, P.W., Holyoak, K.J., Nisbett, R.E., & Oliver, L.M. (1986). Pragmatic versus syntactic approaches to training deductive reasoning. *Cognitive Psychology, 18*, 293–328.

Chomsky, N. (1957). *Syntactic structures*. The Hague: Mouton.

Chomsky, N. (1965). *Aspects of the theory of syntax*. Cambridge, Mass.: MIT Press.

Christensen-Szalanski, J.J.J. & Beach, L.R. (1984). The citation bias: Fad and fashion in the judgement and decision literature. *American Psychologist, 39*, 75–78.

Chrostowski, J.J. & Griggs, R.A. (1985). The effects of problem content, instructions and verbalisation procedure on Wason's selection task. *Current Psychological Research and Reviews, 4*, 99–107.

Clark, H.H. (1969). Linguistic processes in deductive reasoning. *Psychological Review, 76*, 387–404.

Cohen, B. & Murphy, G.L. (1984). Models of concepts. *Cognitive Science, 8*, 27–58.

Cohen, L.J. (1979). On the psychology of prediction: Whose is the fallacy? *Cognition, 7*, 385–407.

Cohen, L.J. (1981). Can human irrationality be experimentally demonstrated? *The Behavioral and Brain Sciences, 4*, 317–370.

Cohen, L.J. (1982). Are people programmed to commit fallacies? Further thought about the interpretation of data on judgement. *Journal for the Theory of Social Behaviour, 12*, 251–274.

Cox, J.R. & Griggs, R.A. (1982). The effects of experience on performance in Wason's selection task. *Memory and Cognition, 10*, 496–502.

Darley, J.M. & Gross, P.H. (1983). A hypothesis-confirming bias in labelling effects. *Journal of Personality and Social Psychology, 44*, 20–33.

de Soto, L.B., London, M., & Handel, L.S. (1965). Social reasoning and spatial paralogic. *Journal of Personality and Social Psychology, 2*, 513–21.

Dickstein, L.S. (1980). Inference errors in deductive reasoning. *Bulletin of the Psychonomic Society, 6*, 414–416.

Dickstein, L.S. (1981). Conversion and possibility in syllogistic reasoning. *Bulletin of the Psychonomic Society, 18*, 229–232.

Dixon, N.F. (1971). *Subliminal perception: The nature of a controversy*. London: McGraw-Hill.

Dixon, N.F. (1981). *Preconscious processing*. Chichester: Wiley.

Doherty, M.E., Mynatt, C.R., Tweney, R.D., & Schiavo, M.D. (1979). Pseudodiagnosticity. *Acta Psychologica*, *43*, 11–21.

Duncker, K. (1945). On problem solving. *Psychological Monographs*, *1945*, *58*, whole no. 270.

Edwards, W. (1977). Use of multi-attribute utility analysis for social decision making. In D.E. Bell, R. L. Keeney & H. Raiffa (Eds.), *Conflicting objectives in decisions*. New York: Wiley.

Ericsson, K.A. & Simon, H.A. (1980). Verbal reports as data. *Psychological Review*, *87*, 215–251.

Ericsson, K.A. & Simon, H.A. (1984). *Protocol analysis: Verbal reports as data*. Cambridge, Mass.: M.I.T. Press.

Evans, J.St.B.T. (1972a). On the problems of interpreting reasoning data: Logical and psychological approaches. *Cognition*, *1*, 373–84.

Evans, J.St.B.T. (1972b). Interpretation and matching bias in a reasoning task. *British Journal of Psychology*, *24*, 193–199.

Evans, J.St.B.T. (1975). On interpreting reasoning data: A reply to Van Duyne. *Cognition*, *3*, 387–390.

Evans, J.St.B.T. (1977). Toward a statistical theory of reasoning. *Quarterly Journal of Experimental Psychology*, *29A*, 297–306.

Evans, J.St.B.T. (1981). A reply to Morris. *British Journal of Psychology*, *72*, 465–468.

Evans, J.St.B.T. (1982). *The psychology of deductive reasoning*. London: Routledge and Kegan Paul.

Evans, J.St.B.T. (1983a). Selective processes in reasoning. In J.St.B.T. Evans (Ed.), *Thinking and reasoning: Psychological approaches*. London: Routledge and Kegan Paul.

Evans, J.St.B.T. (1983b). Linguistic determinants of bias in conditional reasoning. *Quarterly Journal of Experimental Psychology*, *35A*, 635–644.

Evans, J.St.B.T. (1984a). Heuristic and analytic processes in reasoning. *British Journal of Psychology*, *75*, 451–468.

Evans, J.St.B.T. (1984b). In defense of the citation bias in the judgement literature. *American Psychologist*, *39*, 1500–1501.

Evans, J.St.B.T. (1987a). Human biases and computer decision making: a discussion of Jacob et al. *Behaviour and Information Technology*, *6*, 483–487.

Evans, J.St.B.T. (1987b). Reasoning. In H. Belloff & A.M. Coleman (Eds.), *Psychology Survey 6*. Leicester: British Psychological Society.

Evans, J.St.B.T. (1987c). Beliefs and expectations as causes of judgemental bias. In G. Wright & P. Ayton (Eds.), *Judgemental forecasting*. Chichester: Wiley.

Evans, J.St.B.T. (in press). Deductive reasoning in human information processing. In W.H. Newton-Smith & K.V. Wilkes (Eds.), *Modelling the Mind*. Oxford: Oxford University Press.

Evans, J.St.B.T. (1988). The knowledge elicitation problem: A psychological perspective. *Behaviour and Information Technology*, *7*, 111–130.

Evans, J.St.B.T., Ball, L.J., & Brooks, P.G. (1987). Attentional bias and decision order in a reasoning task. *British Journal of Psychology*, *78*, 385–94.

Evans, J.St.B.T., Barston, J.L., & Pollard, P. (1983). On the conflict between logic and belief in syllogistic reasoning. *Memory and Cognition*, *11*, 295–306.

Evans, J.St.B.T. & Bradshaw, H. (1986). Estimating sample size requirements in research design: A study of intuitive statistical judgement. *Current Psychological Research and Reviews*, *5*, 10–19.

Evans, J.St.B.T. & Brooks, P.G. (1981). Competing with reasoning: A test of the working memory hypothesis. *Current Psychological Research*, *1*, 139–147.

Evans, J.St.B.T., Brooks, P.G., & Pollard, P. (1985). Prior beliefs in statistical inference. *British Journal of Psychology*, *76*, 469–477.

Evans, J.St.B.T., Dennis, I., & Sastry, L. (1988). *An interactive decision aid for research design: A preliminary report.* Technical report, Department of Psychology, Plymouth Polytechnic.

Evans, J.St.B.T. & Dusoir, A.E. (1975). *Sample size and subjective probability judgements: A test of Kahneman & Tversky's hypothesis.* Paper read to the Experimental Psychology Society at Oxford University.

Evans, J.St.B.T. & Dusoir, A.E. (1977). Proportionality and sample size as factors in intuitive statistical judgement. *Acta Psychologica, 41,* 129–137.

Evans, J.St.B.T. & Lynch, J.S. (1973). Matching bias in the selection task. *British Journal of Psychology, 64,* 391–397.

Evans, J.St.B.T. & Newstead, S.E. (1977). Language and reasoning: A study of temporal factors. *Cognition, 8,* 265–283.

Evans, J.St.B.T. & Newstead, S.E. (1980). A study of disjunctive reasoning. *Psychological Research, 41,* 373–388.

Evans, J.St.B.T. & Pollard, P. (1982). Statistical judgement: A further test of the representativeness construct. *Acta Psychologica, 51,* 91–103.

Evans, J.St.B.T. & Pollard, P. (1985). Intuitive statistical inferences about normally distributed data. *Acta Psychologica, 60,* 57–71.

Evans, J.St.B.T. & Pollard, P. (1987). *Belief bias and problem complexity in deductive reasoning.* Unpublished manuscript, Plymouth Polytechnic.

Evans, J.St.B.T.& Wason, P.C. (1976). Rationalisation in a reasoning task. *British Journal of Psychology, 63,* 205–212.

Fillenbaum, S. (1975). If: Some uses. *Psychological Research, 37,* 245–60.

Fillenbaum, S. (1976). Inducements: On phrasing and logic of conditional promises, threats and warnings. *Psychological Research, 38,* 231–50.

Fillenbaum, S. (1978). How to do some things with IF. In J.W. Cotton & R.L. Klatzky (Eds.), *Semantic factors in cognition.* Hillsdale, N.J.: Lawrence Erlbaum Associates Inc.

Fischhoff, B. (1975). Hindsight = foresight: The effect of outcome knowledge on judgement under uncertainty. *Journal of Experimental Psychology: Human Perception and Performance, 1,* 288–299.

Fischhoff, B. (1982). For those condemned to study the past: Heuristics and biases in hindsight. In D. Kahneman, P. Slovic, & A. Tversky (Eds.), *Judgement under uncertainty: Heuristics and biases.* Cambridge: Cambridge University Press.

Fischhoff, B., Slovic, P., & Lichtenstein, S. (1977). Knowing with certainty: The appropriateness of extreme confidence. *Journal of Experimental Psychology: Human Perception and Performance, 3,* 552–564.

Fong, G.T., Krantz, D.H., & Nisbett, R.E. (1986). The effects of statistical training on thinking about everyday problems. *Cognitive Psychology, 18,* 253–292.

Gick, M.L. & Holyoak, K.J. (1983). Schema induction and analogical transfer. *Cognitive Psychology, 15,* 1–38.

Golding, E. (1981). *The effect of past experience on problem solving.* Paper presented to the British Psychological Society at Surrey University.

Goodwin, R.Q. & Wason, P.C. (1972). Degrees of insight. *British Journal of Psychology, 63,* 205–212.

Gorman, M.E. (1986). How the possibility of error affects falsification on a task that models scientific problem solving. *British Journal of Psychology, 77,* 85–96.

Gorman, M.E. & Gorman, M.E. (1984). Comparison of disconfirmatory, confirmatory and control strategies on Wason's 2-4-6 task. *Quarterly Journal of Experimental Psychology, 36A,* 629–648.

Gorman, M.E., Gorman, M.E., Latta, R.M., & Cunningham, G. (1984). How disconfirmatory, confirmatory and combined strategies affect group problem solving. *British Journal of Psychology, 75,* 65–97.

Gorman, M.E., Stafford, A., & Gorman, M.E. (1987). Disconfirmation and dual hypotheses on a more difficult version of Wason's 2-4-6 task. *Quarterly Journal of Experimental Psychology*, *39A*, 1–28.

Grice, P. (1975). Logic and conversation. In P. Cole & J.L. Morgan (Eds.), *Studies in syntax. Vol 3: Speech acts*. New York: Academic Press.

Griggs, R.A. (1983). The role of problem content in the selection task and in the THOG problem. In J.St.B.T. Evans (Ed.), *Thinking and reasoning: Psychological approaches*. London: Routledge and Kegan Paul.

Griggs, R.A. (1984). Memory cueing and instructional effects on Wason's selection task. *Current Psychological Research and Reviews*, *3*, 3–10.

Griggs, R.A. & Cox, J.R. (1982). The elusive thematic materials effect in the Wason selection task. *British Journal of Psychology*, *73*, 407–420.

Griggs, R.A. & Cox, J.R. (1983). The effects of problem content and negation on Wason's selection task. *Quarterly Journal of Experimental Psychology*, *35A*, 519–533.

Griggs, R.A. & Newstead, S.E. (1982). The role of problem structure in a deductive reasoning task. *Journal of Experimental Psychology*, *8*, 297–307.

Hayes-Roth, F., Waterman, D.A., & Lenat, D.B. (1983). *Building expert systems*. London: Addison-Wesley.

Henle, M. (1962). On the relation between logic and thinking. *Psychological Review*, *69*, 366–378.

Hitch, G.J. & Baddeley, A.D. (1976). Verbal reasoning and working memory. *Quarterly Journal of Experimental Psychology*, *28*, 603–622.

Hoch, S.J. & Tschirgi, J.E. (1985). Logical knowledge and cue redundancy in deductive reasoning. *Memory & Cognition*, *13*, 453–462.

Holland, J.H., Holyoak, K.J., Nisbett, R.E., & Thagard, P.R. (1986). *Induction: Processes on inference, learning and discovery*. Cambridge, Mass.: M.I.T. Press.

Humphreys, P.C. & McFadden, W. (1980). Experiences with MAUD: Aiding decision structuring versus bootstrapping the decision maker. *Acta Psychologica*, *45*, 51–69.

Humphreys, P.C. & Wishuda, A. (1981). *MAUD4: Decision analysis unit technical report 81–5*. Uxbridge: Brunel University.

Huttenlocher, J. (1968). Constructing spatial images: A strategy in reasoning. *Psychological Review*, *75*, 286–298.

Inhelder, B. & Piaget, J. (1958). *The growth of logical thinking*. New York: Basic Books.

John, R.S., von Winterfeldt, D., & Edwards, W. (1983). The quality of user acceptance of multi-attribute utility analysis performed by computer and analyst. In P. Humphreys, O. Svenson, & A. Vari (Eds.), *Analysing and aiding decision processes*. Amsterdam: North Holland.

Johnson-Laird, P.N. (1983). *Mental models*. Cambridge: Cambridge University Press.

Johnson-Laird, P.N. & Bara, B.G. (1984). Syllogistic inference. *Cognition*, *16*, 1–62.

Johnson-Laird, P.N., Legrenzi, P., & Legrenzi, M.S. (1972). Reasoning and a sense of reality. *British Journal of Psychology*, *63*, 395–400.

Johnson-Laird, P.N. & Steedman, M.J. (1978). The psychology of syllogisms. *Cognitive Psychology*, *10*, 64–69.

Johnson-Laird, P.N. & Tagart, J. (1969). How implication is understood. *American Journal of Psychology*, *2*, 367–373.

Johnson-Laird, P.N. & Wason, P.C. (1970a). A theoretical analysis of insight into a reasoning task. *Cognitive Psychology*, *1*, 134–148.

Johnson-Laird, P.N. & Wason, P.C. (1970b). Insight into a logical relation. *Quarterly Journal of Experimental Psychology*, *22*, 49–61.

Jungermann, H. & Thuring, M. (1987). The use of mental models for generating scenarios. In G. Wright and P. Ayton (Eds.), *Judgemental forecasting*. Chichester: Wiley.

Kahneman, D., Slovic, P., & Tversky, A. (1982). *Judgement under uncertainty: Heuristics and biases*. Cambridge: Cambridge University Press.

Kahneman, D. & Tversky, A. (1972a). *On prediction and judgement*. ORI Research Monograph, 12(4).

Kahneman, D. & Tversky, A. (1972b). Subjective probability: A judgement of representativeness. *Cognitive Psychology*, *3*, 430–454.

Kahneman, D. & Tversky, A. (1973). On the psychology of prediction. *Psychological Review*, *80*, 237–251.

Kahneman, D. & Tversky, A. (1982a). On the study of statistical intuition. *Cognition*, 12, 325–326.

Kahneman, D. & Tversky, A. (1982b). The simulation heuristic. In A. Kahneman, P. Slovic, & A. Tversky (Eds.), *Judgement under uncertainty: Heuristics and biases*. Cambridge: Cambridge University Press.

Kelly, G. (1955). *The psychology of personal constructs* (2 vols) New York: Norton.

Klayman, J. & Ha, Y-W. (1987). Confirmation, disconfirmation and information in hypothesis testing. *Psychological Review*, *94*, 211–228.

Koriat, A., Lichtenstein, S., & Fischhoff, B. (1980). Reasons for confidence. *Journal of Experimental Psychology: Human Learning and Memory*, *6*, 107–118.

Kosslyn, S.M. (1980). *Image and mind*. Cambridge, Mass.: Harvard University Press.

Krauth, J. (1982). Formulation and experimental verification of models in propositional reasoning. *Quarterly Journal of Experimental Psychology*, *34A*, 285–298.

Lemmon, E.J. (1965). *Beginning logic*. London: Nelson.

Levine, M. (1966). Hypothesis behaviour by humans during discrimination learning. *Journal of Experimental Psychology*, *71*, 331–338.

Lewicki, P. (1986). *Nonconscious social information processing*. New York: Academic Press.

Lewicki, P., Hill, T., & Bizot, E. (1988). Acquisition of procedural knowledge about a pattern of stimuli that cannot be articulated. *Cognitive Psychology*, *20*, 24–37.

Lichtenstein, S. & Fischhoff, B. (1980). Training for calibration. *Organisational Behaviour and Human Performance*, *26*, 149–171.

Lichtenstein, S., Fischhoff, B., & Phillips, L.D. (1982). Calibration of probabilities: The state of the art to 1980. In D. Kahneman, P. Slovic, & A. Tversky (Eds.), *Judgement under uncertainty: Heuristics and biases*. Cambridge: Cambridge University Press.

Lichtenstein, S., Slovic, P., Fischhoff, B., & Layman, M. (1978). Judged frequency of lethal events. *Journal of Experimental Psychology: Human Learning and Memory*, *4*, 551–578.

Lopes, L.L. (1987). Procedural debiasing. *Acta Psychologica*, *64*, 167–185.

Lord, C., Ross, L., & Lepper, M.R. (1979). Biased assimilation and attitude polarisation: The effect of prior theories on subsequently considered evidence. *Journal of Personality and Social Psychology*, *37*, 2098–2109.

Luchins, A.S. & Luchins, E.H. (1950). New experimental attempts at preventing mechanisation in problem solving. *Journal of General Psychology*, *42*, 279–297.

Manktelow, K.I. & Evans, J.St.B.T. (1979). Facilitation of reasoning by realism: Effect or non-effect? *British Journal of Psychology*, *70*, 477–488.

Marcus, S.L. & Rips, L.J. (1979). Conditional reasoning. *Journal of Verbal Learning and Verbal Behavior*, *18*, 199–233.

Mathews, R.C., Buss, R.R., Chinn, R., & Stanley, W.B. (1988). The role of explicit and implicit learning processes in concept discovery. *Quarterly Journal of Experimental Psychology*, *40A*, 135–165.

Metcalfe, J. & Wiebe, D. (1987). Intuition in insight and noninsight problem solving. *Memory & Cognition*, *15*, 238–246.

Miller, G.A. (1967). *The psychology of communication* (Chapter 7). New York: Basic Books.

Morris, P.E. (1981). Why Evans is wrong in criticising introspective reports of subject strategies. *British Journal of Psychology*, *72*, 465–468.

Mynatt, C.R., Doherty, M.E., & Tweney, R.D. (1977). Confirmation bias in a simulated research environment: An experimental study of scientific inference. *Quarterly Journal of Experimental Psychology*, *24*, 326–329.

Mynatt, C.R., Doherty, M.E., & Tweney, R.D. (1978). Consequences of confirmation and disconfirmation in a simulated research environment. *Quarterly Journal of Experimental Psychology*, *30*, 85–96.

Newell, A. & Simon, H.A. (1972). *Human problem solving*. Englewood Cliffs, N.J.: Prentice-Hall.

Newstead, S.E., Griggs, R.A., & Chrostowski, J.J. (1984). Reasoning with realistic disjunctives. *Quarterly Journal of Experimental Psychology*, *36A*, 611–627.

Newstead, S.E., Manktelow, K.I., & Evans, J.St.B.T. (1982). The role of imagery in the representation of linear orderings. *Current Psychological Research*, *2*, 21–32.

Nickerson, R.S., Perkins, D.N., & Smith, E.E. (1985). *The teaching of thinking*. Hillsdale, N.J.: Lawrence Erlbaum Associates Inc.

Nisbett, R.E., Krantz, D.H., Jepson, D.H., & Kunda, Z. (1983). The use of statistical heuristics in everyday inductive reasoning. *Psychological Review*, *90*, 339–363.

Nisbett, R. & Ross, L. (1980). *Human inference: Strategies and shortcomings of social judgement*. Englewood Cliffs, N.J.: Prentice-Hall.

Nisbett, R.E. & Wilson, T.D. (1977). Telling more than we can know: Verbal reports on mental processes. *Psychological Review*, *84*, 231–295.

Norman, D.A. & Draper, S.W. (1986). *User centered system design*. Hillsdale, N.J.: Lawrence Erlbaum Associates Inc.

Oakhill, J. & Johnson-Laird, P.N. (1985a). Rationality, memory and the search for counterexamples. *Cognition*, *20*, 79–94.

Oakhill, J. & Johnson-Laird, P.N. (1985b). The effect of belief on the spontaneous production of syllogistic conclusions. *Quarterly Journal of Experimental Psychology*, *37A*, 553–570.

Olson, C.L. (1976). Some apparent violations of the representativeness heuristic in human judgement. *Journal of Experimental Psychology: Human Perception and Performance*, *2*, 599–608.

Peterson, C.R. & Beach, L.R. (1967). Man as an intuitive statistician. *Psychological Bulletin*, *68*, 29–46.

Phillips, L.D. (1987). On the adequacy of judgemental forecasts. In G. Wright and P.Ayton (Eds.), *Judgemental forecasting*. Chichester: Wiley.

Platt, J.R. (1964). Strong inference. *Science*, *146*, 347–53.

Pollard, P. (1979). *Human reasoning: Logical and nonlogical explanations*. Unpublished Ph.D. thesis, Plymouth Polytechnic.

Pollard, P. (1982). Human reasoning: Some possible effects of availability. *Cognition*, *12*, 65–96.

Pollard, P. & Evans, J.St.B.T. (1980). The influence of logic on conditional reasoning performance. *Quarterly Journal of Experimental Psychology*, *32*, 605–24.

Pollard, P. & Evans, J.St.B.T. (1981). The effect of prior beliefs in reasoning: An associational interpretation. *British Journal of Psychology*, *72*, 73–82.

Pollard, P. & Evans, J.St.B.T. (1987). On the relationship between content and context effects in reasoning. *American Journal of Psychology*, *100*, 41–60.

Popper, K.R. (1959). *The logic of scientific discovery*. London: Hutchinson.

Popper, K.R. (1962). *Conjectures and refutations*. London: Hutchinson.

Quinton, G. & Fellows, S.B.J. (1975). "Perceptual" strategies in the solving of three term series problems. *British Journal of Psychology*, *66*, 69–78.

Reber, A.S. (1976). Implicit learning of synthetic languages: The role of instructional set. *Journal of Experimental Psychology: Human Learning and Memory*, *2*, 88–94.

Reber, A.S., Kassin, S.M., Lewis, S., & Cantor, G. (1980). On the relationship between implicit and explicit modes in the learning of a complex rule struture. *Journal of Experimental Psychology: Human Learning and Memory*, *6*, 492–502.

Reich, S.S. & Ruth, P. (1982). Wason's selection task: Verification, falsification and matching. *British Journal of Psychology*, 395–405.

Revlin, R., Leirer, V., Yopp, H., & Yopp, R. (1980). The belief bias effect in formal reasoning: The influence of knowledge on logic. *Memory and Cognition*, *8*, 584–592.

Revlis, R. (1975a). Syllogistic reasoning: Logical decisions from a complex data base. In R.J. Falmagne (Ed.), Reasoning: Representation and process. New York: Wiley.

Revlis, R. (1975b). Two models of syllogistic inference: Feature selection and conversion. *Journal of Verbal Learning and Verbal Behavior*, *14*, 180–195.

Richardson, J.T.E. (1987). The role of mental imagery in models of transitive inference. *British Journal of Psychology*, *78*, 189–203.

Rips, L.J. (1983). Cognitive processes in propositional reasoning. *Psychological Review*, *90*, 38–71.

Rips, L.J. & Marcus, S.L. (1977). Suppositions and the analysis of conditional sentences. In M.A. Just & P.A. Carpenter (Eds.), *Cognitive processes in comprehension*. New York: Wiley.

Rumelhart, D.E. (1980). Schemata: The building blocks of cognition. In R.J. Spiro, B.C. Bruce, & W.F. Brewer (Eds.), *Theoretical issues in reading comprehension*. Hillsdale, N.J.: Lawrence Erlbaum Associates Inc.

Schneider, W. & Shiffrin, R.M. (1977). Controlled and automatic human information processing I: Detection, search and attention. *Psychological Review*, *84*, 1–66.

Shaver, P., Pierson, L., & Lang, S. (1975). Converging evidence for the functional significance of imagery in problem solving. *Cognition*, *3*, 395–7.

Shiffrin, R.M. & Schneider, W. (1977). Controlled and automatic human information processing II: Perceptual learning, automatic attending and a general theory. *Psychological Review*, *84*, 127–189.

Slovic, P., Fischhoff, B., & Lichtenstein, S. (1977). Behavioral decision theory. *Annual Review of Psychology*, *228*, 1–39.

Sperber, D. & Wilson, D. (1986). *Relevance*. Oxford: Basil Blackwell.

Staudenmayer, H. (1975). Understanding conditional reasoning with meaningful propositions. In R.J. Falmagne (Ed.), *Reasoning: Representation and process*. New York: Wiley.

Sternberg, R.J. (1980). Representation and process in linear syllogistic reasoning. *Journal of Experimental Psychology: General*, *109*, 119–159.

Taylor, S.E. & Thompson, S.C. (1982). Stalking the elusive "vividness" effect. *Psychological Review*, *89*, 155–181.

Tversky, A. & Kahneman, D. (1971). The belief in the "law of small numbers". *Psychological Bulletin*, *76*, 105–110.

Tversky, A. & Kahneman, D. (1973). Availability: A heuristic for judging frequency and probability. *Cognitive Psychology*, *5*, 207–232.

Tversky, A. & Kahneman, D. (1980). Causal schemata in judgements under uncertainty. In M. Fishbein (Ed.), *Progress in social psychology*. Hillsdale, N.J.: Lawrence Erlbaum Associates Inc.

Tweney, R.D., Doherty, M.E., & Mynatt, C.R. (1981). *On scientific thinking*. New York: Columbia University Press.

Tweney, R.D., Doherty, M.E., Warner, W.J., & Pliske, D.B. (1980). Strategies of rule discovery in an inference task. *Quarterly Journal of Experimental Psychology*, *32*, 109–24.

Valentine, E.R. (1985). The effect of instructions on performance in the Wason selection task. *Current Psychological Research and Reviews*, *4*, 214–223.

Van Duyne, P.C. (1976). Necessity and contingency in reasoning. *Acta Psychologica*, *40*, 85–101.

von Neumann, J. & Morgenstern, O. (1947). *Theory of games and economic behavior*. Princeton, N.J.: Princeton University Press.

von Winterfeldt, D. & Edwards, W. (1986). *Decision analysis and behavioural research*. Cambridge: Cambridge University Press.

Wason, P.C. (1960). On the failure to eliminate hypotheses in a conceptual task. *Quarterly Journal of Experimental Psychology*, *12*, 129–140.

Wason, P.C. (1966). Reasoning. In B.M. Foss (Ed.), *New horizons in psychology I*. Harmandsworth: Penguin.

Wason, P.C. (1967). On the failure to eliminate hypotheses: A second look. In P.C. Wason & P.N. Johnson-Laird (Eds.), *Thinking and reasoning*. Harmandsworth: Penguin.

Wason, P.C. (1969). Regression in reasoning? *British Journal of Psychology*, *60*, 471–480.

Wason, P.C. (1983). Realism and rationality in the selection task. In J.St.B.T. Evans (Ed.), *Thinking and reasoning: Psychological approaches*. London: Routledge and Kegan Paul.

Wason, P.C. & Brooks, P.G. (1979). THOG: The anatomy of a problem. *Psychological Research*, *41*, 79–90.

Wason, P.C. & Evans, J.St.B.T. (1975). Dual processes in reasoning? *Cognition*, *3*, 141–154.

Wason, P.C. & Golding, E. (1974). The language of inconsistency. *British Journal of Psychology*, *65*, 537–546.

Wason, P.C. & Green, D. (1984). Reasoning and mental representation. *Quarterly Journal of Experimental Psychology*, *36A*, 597–610.

Wason, P.C. & Johnson-Laird, P.N. (1970). A conflict between selecting and evaluation of information in an inferential task. *British Journal of Psychology*, *61*, 509–515.

Wason, P.C. & Johnson-Laird, P.N. (1972). *Psychology of reasoning: Structure and content*. London: Batsford.

Wason, P.C. & Shapiro, D. (1971). Natural and contrived experience in a reasoning problem. *Quarterly Journal of Experimental Psychology*, *23*, 63–71.

Wetherick, N.E. (1962). Eliminative and enumerative behaviour in a conceptual task. *Quarterly Journal of Experimental Psychology*, *14*, 246–249.

White, P.A. (1988). Knowing more than we can tell: "Introspective access" and causal report accuracy 10 years later. *British Journal of Psychology*, *79*, 13–46.

Wilkins, M.C. (1928). *The effect of changed material on the ability to do formal syllogistic reasoning*. Archives of Psychology, New York, No.102.

Yachanin, S.A. (1986). Facilitation in Wason's selection task: Contents and instructions. *Current Psychological Research and Reviews*, *5*, 20–29.

Yachanin, S.A. & Tweney, R.D. (1982). The effect of thematic content on cognitive strategies in the four-card selection task. *Bulletin of the Psychonomic Society*, *19*, 87–90.

Author Index

Subject Index